What peo
about this ..

CW01667589

It's an unsettling and tragic truth that too many women find themselves subjected by way of emotional and/or physical means by their abusers.

Here five very courageous ladies share their respective experiences.

Highlighting the manipulative, abusive and controlling behaviour that at first almost goes unnoticed but eventually and insidiously becomes all-encompassing.

An invaluable read for all teenage girls and indeed a valuable insight for women of any age.

Karen Williams OBE – Founder of the Buddy Bag Foundation

As a detective in a Major Incident Team I have been involved in many murder investigations. I was appalled by the number of murders committed by partners and ex partners. What is certain is that we need to address domestic abuse at the very start. Rie Pearson highlights behaviours that lead to abuse. The insidious, under the radar stuff that can sometime pass as caring, when it's really control. What a brilliant way to raise awareness to save lives.

Rie Pearson highlights behaviours that lead to abuse and in some cases ultimately death."

James Harris, retired Major Incident Team Detective, Humberside Police

Brilliant insight into the degrading, debilitating and tragic world of domestic abuse. Told through the eyes of five victims of appalling emotional and physical harm, Rie Pearson draws upon her many years of experience as a police officer to provide expert guidance designed to help and protect those entering into intimate relationships, particularly teenage girls. Highly recommend.

Dr Paul Davison. Former Chief Superintendent, Humberside Police.

This should be a 'go to resource' for those working with women who have experienced domestic abuse, looking to 'move on' with new confidence. And, if you have lived with violence and felt silenced for too long this is the book where you can hear voices showing that there is life to be lived free from abuse. Real, authentic experiences yet giving hope.

The author synthesises professional experience with an understanding of the issue which is revealed in these personal anecdotes.

Louise Brown. Bed, M.A. Retired Director of Wear Valley Women's Aid. Senior practitioner with specialism in the impact on children and young people. Trained and raised awareness with CAB and Police. Community Support to Magistrates.

Since meeting Rie Pearson online and chats over WhatsApp I have learnt so much about this topic.

Her book is a collection of short stories from women who have experienced abuse. Rie references each paragraph and outlines the abusive behaviour from the red flags at the beginning of the relationship. Five chilling accounts from brave ladies willing to share their experiences to help others.

Thank you, Rie for opening my eyes. This is such an important message to share not only with our daughters but also with our sons.

Claire Owen. The Soberholic - coaches ambitious but frazzled women to stop relying on alcohol to fuel their busy lives.

This important, compelling book is a must-read for anyone who cares about women, our daughters, sisters, mums and friends. With great insight sparked by a career at the sharp end, Rie has crafted stories that will stay with the reader long after the cover is closed on first reading. A scourge of domestic violence looms too large in our society and giving young women the tools to recognise and act decisively on it is a vital step forward as Be Kind, No Excuses and its passion to protect, educate and change behaviour shows.

Linda Aitchison, Buddy Bag Foundation volunteer, writer and journalist.

Be Kind – No Excuses

A guide to help teenage girls recognise abusive behaviours in intimate relationships

Rie Pearson

ISBN 978-1-8383689-1-3

Published by CP Print
18 Provident Street
Pelton Lane Ends Chester-le-Street
DH2 1NS

www.riepearson.com

A guide for teenage girls in new relationships...

- ✓ *What to accept and whatnot to accept in an intimate relationship.*
- ✓ *How to stay safe. A truthful, open, and honest guide for teenage girls.*

The UN office on Drugs and Crime reported in 2019 that globally, more than 30,000 women were murdered by their partner or former partner.

So, at least 82 per day!

Let's learn how to avoid abusers and being dead....

Dedication.

To my children. Thank you.

There. Their. They're.

Contents

What people are saying about this book 1
Introduction 13
Health Warning 13
How to use the book 14

Stories – 15

Story One: Listen to your gut! 17
Story Two: Value yourself. 41
Story Three: There is No Need for Speed 61
Story Four: Believe in Yourself 73
Story Five: Be Brave for Yourself, Not for Others 85
Authors note about this story 90

Additional Resources – 93

Self Esteem 95
How we should honour ourselves 95
Personal Affirmations 97
Gratitude is an Attitude 99
Staying Safe 100
Things that we know are very dangerous when someone is in an abusive relationship 101
Maslow's Hierarchy of Needs 102
Definitions 103
Additional Support 107
About the Author 108

Introduction

Health Warning

The five stories you are about to read are all true and written by the person in the story who is the victim of domestic abuse.

They are not easy to read because they are about how a person can be horrible to someone they say they love. Some parts are frightening. Mostly, they are incredibly sad.

This book is written with teenage heterosexual girls in mind. If you are a gay or bi boy, then it may also help you. The reason for this is, the largest group of reported domestic violence sufferers are female and the perpetrators are male.

In my personal experience, all victims I worked with were female, and the offenders were male. I am not saying abuse does not happen in other relationships, just in my personal journey helping victims and investigating offenders, I've never encountered a male who was at high* risk from a female.

I have had the privilege to encounter some amazing women in my life, and some of them have very kindly contributed to this book. I'd like to thank them all from my heart for going through the difficult and upsetting process of putting their stories in to words. It is sometimes cathartic, sometimes not. A few more women have offered to write their stories, but when it came to it, they were unable to due to the amount of upset it caused them.

**High risk being likely to die or be seriously harmed.*

That is an indication of the pain caused, even, in some cases, years after the abusive relationship has ended.

The book is a guide and reference book. In the telling of each story, I have marked within the text to help you recognize different behaviours that are indicative of abuse. We will analyse these behaviours in paragraphs after each story and hopefully that will make it easier for you to follow.

I have chosen stories from women who have different backgrounds and different lifestyles. Domestic violence knows no boundaries and I wanted that to be shown in the telling.

This book is written to help you avoid abusive relationships by recognising behaviours in the early stages!

How to use the book

This book is a guide. There are five stories. All true. Each story is followed by Notes. The numbers throughout each story relate to the corroborating Notes.

I have included a short description of each person who has written her story.

One of the stories might just resonate with you. Maybe all of them will. Most of them cover a variety of abusive behaviours.

Some abusive behaviours may appear, at first, to be 'caring' behaviours. This book should help you clarify the difference between 'caring' and 'control'.

Stories

Affirmation

I believe in Me
and what
I am capable of.

Story One:
Listen to your gut!

The author: The lady who wrote this story is a professional and strong business woman.

The first time I saw him, I think I fell in love. I was sat at a typical Italian bar on a hot summer's afternoon when I noticed a really good looking guy. He had long, dark, curly hair, his skin was tanned and amazing eyes that seemed to look deep into your soul. He was stood, leaning casually at the entrance to the bar looking out and chatting to other locals. With a small beer in one hand, the other he was teasingly stroking his stomach. Being warm, only a few buttons of his crisp white shirt were done up, so I had a good view of his golden abs and chest. His jeans and shoes were designer and his jewellery was minimal yet effective. He had such a sexy aura to him, and I was very intrigued. I was a 30-year-old single mum at the time, not looking for a serious relationship but open to suggestions. He had caught my eye and I had caught his.

It wasn't until a few days later that I saw him again, in a different bar, looking just as good and smelling even better. As he came in a friend of mine said hi to him and they started chatting, so they obviously knew each other. After he had moved on to another group of people I inquired as to who he was, and my friend informed me that he was a relative of hers. A 38-year- old entrepreneur who was separated and was living with his teenage daughter.[1]

This intrigued and impressed me even more so after a few more flirty glances between us I offered to buy him a drink. We hit it off straight away, chatting and flirting with each other for the rest of the evening. When it was closing time, he walked over to his van and called me over and in private he declared that he was divorced and would like my number so we could go out sometime. Of course I agreed but I wanted to play it cool so I told him that I was quite a busy person with being a mum and work and jokingly, so as not to seem rude, asked him not to harass me with calls. As we said goodbye and I walked away he phoned. I thought that was cute and brave like he couldn't wait to speak to me. Looking back, that was the first time he purposefully crossed a boundary, jokingly or not, and the harassment began.[2]

The next day he took me out for a ride on his motorbike and kissed me on the lips when he helped me off and I let him. For a few weeks we went out, spoke on the phone, exchanged messages and it was fun, it made me feel wanted

---

1. *When I hear that a man has residence (formerly known as "custody") of his children I often consider how this has come about.*
Please note, not all men are abusers, and some women are, and occasionally, children go to live with their dads. However, in cases where abuse is present, a woman, knowing the level of threat and danger, will know that it is safer for the children, to leave them with their father.
Please don't judge when you come across this, but try to understand, horrible though it is.
This may seem extreme, as he is abusive, but most abused women know the risk of separation, i.e. the increased risk of her and her children being murdered.
It is often safer to let the abuser care for the children because this is a better choice than the risk of him murdering them if they are "taken away"
2. *In all relationships we set boundaries. Most people respect and acknowledge those limits. The phone call in this story literally, was 'outed' him as an abuser.*
Stepping over a boundary is clear indication one person believes themselves to be more important than another person.

and desired. During that time we had a few more kisses but we did a lot of talking. I told him about my own father and my previous partner and how wary I was of an abusive relationship.[3]

He told me about how his ex-wife had left him and his daughter, about his unhappy marriage to a woman who only wanted to have fun and never take responsibility, and about how she had run away with another man.[4]

I thought that her loss was my gain. I began to think that I would be so different to her, I would treat this guy right. He would surprise me by picking me up from work in his car, showing up unexpected at my door on his motorbike or happen to be driving by the train station in his work van.[5]

I was overwhelmed with all the attention and his calm manner. We spoke for hours about his travels and how he had been to Taiwan, travelled around Europe and his various businesses.

On our very first night together he whispered to me that he wanted me to be the mother of all his children. All? I

---

3. Previous abusive relationships.
When we get to know someone, it is natural to share our past. To discuss what we want in life, and what we don't want.
When we first meet someone, it is new and exciting. We bare our souls to them.
When that person is a perpetrator, they will save up all this information. They will identify our vulnerabilities and keep them for later.
4. Beware the man who maligns his ex wife or girlfriend. He gives us one side of the story. His side. His ex may well have been a nightmare, but until you know for sure, be careful. It could well be, down the line, you are the ex he's talking about.
This is what I call 'Poor me syndrome'. He wants you to feel sorry for him and 'take his side'. Try to resist being sucked in to.
5. There's a line between attention and stalking. Someone who turns up 'accidentally' isn't turning up accidentally. Showing up unexpected at your door is not a good sign. Apart from being rude, it is an indication he is checking up on you and who you are with, and making sure you are home, if that is where you said you'd be. Stalking is a HIGH RISK FACTOR in domestic murder.

giggled it off but I thought that was lovely. I was getting a bit of hassle from my son's father at the time and him saying that really made me feel appreciated and loved. It would become a common topic for him right from the first month. I began to imagine my own nice big family, with an amazing guy, perfection.[6]

At the time I was working in Rome for a company teaching English to Italian businesspeople and also worked freelance from home. I was earning good money and was extremely happy with my work. During the first few weeks of seeing each other he would take me to dinner and show me off to his friends which made me feel like the most important woman in the world.[7]

My family lived back in the UK and although I had many friends, this attention was just what I needed. I found it really sweet the way he would show up when I was out with friends and take me home, the way he would call me umpteen times a day asking what I was doing and showing an interest in my day.[8, 9]

We had been together for about a month when one evening I had told him I would be working as I had a male

---

6. *"I want you to have my babies", "all his children".*
Couple of things here. How long into an intimate relationship do you think it is appropriate to bring up the subject of starting a family? There is no wrong or right answer to that. I don't think it is on the first night of passion, personally.
Also, "my" and "his". Not "our" children?? This is an indication this man is all about himself.
7. *Showing someone off to their friends is not a good thing. You are not a trophy or a possession, or eye-candy. You are not there to be displayed like an exhibit.*
8. *Showing up when you are out with friends is an indicator this person is possessive and jealous. He is checking up on you and making sure you're not with another man.*
9. *Constant phone calls. It is lovely to feel loved, but this is not love. It is keeping tabs on you to make sure you are exactly where you said you would be!*

DJ friend coming round as we were working on the lyric some songs. He looked offended and expressed his sadness that I would want to spend time with another man then left in a mood.[10]

During the writing session I had a few calls from him which became uncomfortable in the presence of my client.[9]

I tried to reassure him that it was purely work over and over. Looking back, my gut feeling was that of discomfort, but I brushed that aside and the attention felt good. I thought how serious he must be about me if he felt that jealous. During that session he called several times to the point where my client felt awkward and wanted to leave. After convincing him to stay and complete our session I turned off my phone. A short while later there was a loud banging at the front door. When I opened it, I found a close friend of his stood at the door, peering straight at the table, wanting to know who my male friend was and if he was disturbing something?[11]

I was in shock that he had sent, what I know now to be, one of his flying monkeys' round to check up on me. I felt violated and untrusted. This was the very first time I had the gut feeling that something wasn't right, but I refused the thought once he had apologised for not trusting me. Unfortunately, his wife leaving him had left scars on him,

---

10. If someone tells you it is natural for a man to be jealous of another man you choose to spend time with, they are wrong. We are different genders, there are more than two genders and who we work with is irrelevant when it comes to gender. If that puts your boyfriend in to a mood, call him out on it. "In a mood" is petulant and childish.

Being jealous is not a positive. No matter how they portray it in the soaps.

11. Using others to perpetrate abuse is common. It helps the perpetrator feel one step removed, and he can say it wasn't him. Of course, this is nonsense, and he's 100% keeping an eye on you.

own, we were even more destined to be nething didn't fit![12]

om a broken home where my mother had been a victim of domestic violence. My memories of that time are not all pleasant.[13]

The father of my first child had an addiction. He worked in the city for a software company and hid it well. I tried to help him but concluded that, with a small child to look after, it really wasn't worth the hassle. With addiction comes mood swings and aggression. As I had experienced this as a child, I didn't want my own son to go through the same things so after just two years we started to separate.[14]

It was a messy split and I felt like a failure. I hadn't saved my son's dad from addiction, the relationship or any money and I hit a very low point.[15]

My child was the only thing that kept me going. I managed to build up my career and with the help of friends,

---

12. Past experiences and excuses.
Anyone who has experienced the breakup of a relationship is likely to have emotional scars and be wary. Be careful that, only knowing one side of the story, that this isn't going to become an excuse for inexcusable behaviour.
We can all be vulnerable, but we are hellish more vulnerable when we are dating a narcissist.
13. I want to add here about experience in our childhood home. I could write a separate book about this!
Violence in a home is child abuse. Children see, hear, feel violence. If a man is abusing the mother, regardless of whether the children are in the room or building, this is child abuse.
Forget "Well, he'd never hurt the kids". He already did!
Coming from a violent home does not mean you will end up in a violent relationship. You are most likely determined NOT to get involved in a violent relationship. But just be mindful, because of this extra caution, you will be vulnerable, and perpetrators are attracted to vulnerability.
14. This story is written by a strong, intelligent and independent woman
Anyone can end up being abused! It is no judgement. It is a fact.
15. Addiction is a BASTARD! Remember, you are not qualified (unless you actually are) to SAVE someone from themselves. Don't try. It doesn't work. And if the abuser asks you to save them, and uses that as a way to apologise for abusive behaviour, do not accept the apology, because it isn't an apology.

good weather, food and wine I was soon blossoming into a successful single mother. I needed no one and felt confident, invincible, and was really enjoying life. When I met him it just seemed like the icing on the cake. I was old enough to know that this was the man for me, and I was the woman for him. If only we had met earlier...I had that butterfly feeling in my stomach whenever I saw him, my appetite had come back and things were looking like a fairy tale ending. We could end there and say they lived happily ever after, except they didn't! What came next was 13 years of emotional, verbal, and financial abuse with the odd eruption of violence here and there just to make sure I knew who was boss.[16]

Writing this is hard because it forces me to recall events that I would happily forget. It is a cause of pain. It is hard putting those deeply hidden feelings on to paper in the form of lines and squiggles. I believe writing this will have two beneficial effects; one is a form of self-counselling as I have never spoken to a therapist. The second is the hope of creating awareness among young women of what signs to recognise in an abuser, what not to do and how important it is to listen to your gut feeling and trust it when you have that feeling that something isn't quite right.

At the time we started dating I was, I thought, a strong woman. I was a single mother in a foreign country with a well-

---

16. Not all domestic violence is physical. Because you aren't being punched, doesn't mean you aren't in an abusive relationship. Women have said to me "I wish he'd just punch me and get it over with". Emotional and psychological abuse is just as real as physical abuse.

Granted, and I have to point this out, you don't bleed to death from being called a "silly fat cow" or "stupid bitch" or whatever.

But if the relentless threat of a possible punch or good hiding is always hanging in the air, the emotional strain is immense.

paid job that I enjoyed. My mother had come out of a violent marriage with two small children and was my role model. She gave me the strength and courage to know that if I counted on myself and believed in myself, I could achieve anything.

Back in the 80's, when I was a child, there was no counselling for children who were victims of domestic violence so I had carried a lot of emotional baggage but pushed it deep down. Along with other emotional scars I had picked up during my wild teenage years, I had many suppressed emotions that I thought I was over.

I was a fulltime working mother who was financially independent and who had overcome a very troubled relationship with all it is mood swings and walking on eggshells. I had friends, holidays abroad with my son, day trips, we were having fun.[17]

The reason I reiterate what a strong, independent woman I was is because you would think that a perpetrator would be looking for someone weak, easy to manipulate, even a mess! Surly that would be the best tactic? Showering the victim with gifts, support and a sprinkling of emotional manipulation! Yes, there is that of course, but not only...there is the trophy, the prize. I have since come to realise the he was a narcissist and that I had all the traits that attracts this type of person.[18]

---

17. Walking on eggshells...
If you feel you need to be careful (not in a good way) about what you say and do so as not to upset your boyfriend, you need to think hard about whether you can do this over a prolonged period and whether this person is right for you (he's not!). Walking on eggshells is a form of emotional abuse.
18. Narcissist – Definition noun A person who has an excessive interest in or admiration of themselves. "narcissists think the world revolves around them"

Narcissists look for someone who completes them and so being strong, financially secure, successful and attractive, often draw a bad person to a good one. During those first months, unbeknown to me, he would use a number of manipulative tactics such as isolation[19] and the silent treatment,[20] making jokes when they were really insults,[21] gaslighting and more.[22]

I believe now that I was his new 'designer' girlfriend to match his designer jeans and sunglasses.[23]

Perpetrators will catch your eye and seduce. If it works out for them, great, if not there are other seductive eye contacts,

---

19. *Isolation is a high risk factor for victims. A perpetrator will alienate you from your friends. He'll say, for example, "I don't like Katie. I think she's jealous of me now I'm with you".*
"Why do you want to go out with your friends? Why cannot we just have a cosy night in just the two of us?" Lots of things, to divide you from your friends and family. To have you all to himself.
Eventually you could find yourself without friends, and totally dependent on him for your emotional wellbeing, which is exactly where he wants you to be.
20. *The silent treatment. Making you feel bad for something he has done that he shouldn't have. Making you sad for a bad behaviour he has expressed. For example: You want a night out with the girls. He's not happy. He decides to stop speaking to you. All this because your friends invited you somewhere. And you haven't even been yet!*
While I'm on the subject...
The silent treatment includes withholding sex. Yes, he will refuse to have sex with you to cause you more hurt. He could be right there with a boner and he'll knock you back because he's treating you with contempt.
21. *Making jokes that are really insults, and then you are accused of 'Taking things the wrong way', 'being too sensitive' or 'misunderstanding'. All the things you are not, and yes, he is being cruel.*
If someone does or says something that makes you feel bad about yourself, you need to think about why that person is behaving that way.
22. *Gaslighting.*
Gaslighting is a form of brainwashing and manipulation. You will begin to doubt yourself.
For example: You'll set a time to meet, and they'll turn up 30 minutes later and absolutely convince you that you are the one with the wrong time.
That's a 'gentle' example, they are usually much worse.
23. *A perpetrator of abuse will go from relationship to relationship. They don't care how many. The narcissist has no empathy for the trail of destruction they leave in their wake. Just be aware that someone who is getting involved with you, who says negative things about their exs, is probably not a great choice for your future happiness.*

half smiles and superiority body language flirting going on elsewhere for him to pursue.[24]

The guy was also an artist, which, made him appealing and mysterious. He had an eye for detail. During those first few months of dating we talked about life, it is ups and downs, and how it had affected us differently, yet destiny had brought us together. He told me about his crazy ex-wife who had had various affairs and who had abandoned him and his daughter.[4]

I confided in him about my son's father, about how he had treated me, how I had to make sure the house was clean and tidy when he got back from work, how he complained his work shirts weren't ironed properly. Of course, this new prince charming that I had before me was so much more relaxed. He had a cleaner so I wouldn't have to worry about that for a start! He explained that his air of superiority and confidence came from his stint in the army where he had also learnt to iron, sew, and cook too. He told me about how his ex-wife had always complained when he would occasionally go out with his friends, that she would get hysterical when he got back and how his daughter has suffered due to this unstable relationship.[4]

His ex had enjoyed life too much to have other children and had denied him his dream of having a large family. We spoke about how both of our fathers were violent men and I told him about my fear of violence. Of course, this

24. *Superiority body language. Flirting.*
An abusive person will focus their attention on you, and then, switch away, making you feel slightly confused. They don't value you and will often talk over the top of you. You may have heard this described as "mansplaining".

prince charming I had before me, would never lay hands on a woman and he repeated that over, just to make sure I knew that he would never hurt a woman. When I asked why she had not taken her daughter he said that nobody comes between him and his child and he would repeat that over and over, in many different ways, just so I knew that.[1]

I liked his hands, they were big and strong, artistic and kind. Hands I would hold close to me and fall asleep against. Hands that he promised would never hurt a woman. Once they did, I would never look at his hands the same way again.

During these initial months there were plenty of signs, that with hindsight, I would now suggest you walk away from. The times he gave me the silent treatment, his condescending tone, the asymmetric expressions, sighs, smirks and frowns when I said or did something that he didn't agree with. The initial grooming, tricking, misleading and lying behaviour.[25]

The times he forgot his wallet, the time he persuaded me to pay one of his contactors on his behalf. The times he would call at random times asking where I was, what I was doing and who I was with. The promises, the look of utter love in his eyes when he spoke in his soft, deep Italian voice, his disappointment if I had made plans that didn't involve him. All in the first few months.

The child that needed to please had been stirred within me and at that time I believed that if only this man had the

---

25. *Grooming is a process. It can take days. It can take years. It starts out as targeted behaviour. Being lovely, being kind. Manipulating you into a position where you feel loved and wanted. But it is a process to get you to where the perpetrator wants you to be.*
Of course, not all kind people are doing this, they are just being kind (like normal, non-abusive people). That's why you need to be vigilant of the signs.

right woman he would overcome his hurt, insecurities and feeling of abandonment that his ex-wife had left him with. I felt wanted and needed by a successful older man, a single father who had complex needs and was sexy.[26]

About three months into the relationship I had an anonymous call which I answered. It was a very stern Italian woman who asked who I was. I could immediately make out she was not a happy woman, but I stayed calm and went on to inform her, very professionally, that she had called me therefore she should introduce herself first. She claimed to be his wife and started to ramble on about how he was her husband, how dare I and to stay away. She got almost hysterical as you would expect a wife to be who had just found a woman's number and messages on her husband's phone. I don't remember her exact words, I was in my kitchen is all I recall. I often go into fight, flight or freeze mode when put in a challenging situation and this was one of them. It was a racing heart, sweaty palms type moment. I had no conversation with this woman other that saying something like she must have reached the wrong person, then hung up in disbelief.

My mind was full of doubts and questions but that was all put to rest once I had had chance to talk to him about it. For so long she had done exactly as she had pleased but now that he was doing his own thing, she obviously didn't like it. The tables were turned. He admitted that he hadn't

26. *In this story, the writer is betrayed by her own kindness and empathy. Her vulnerabilities are on display and the narcissist sees this and it completes him. Targeting those traits he does not possess himself is his key motivation. He finds someone with empathy and kindness and is attracted. Like an addiction.*

been completely honest with me though. They had, in fact, divorced years before but he had taken her back a year or so ago for the sake of their daughter. They had owned two clothes shops, one in the hometown and one where she was living.[27]

He explained that they had often gone there for the summer but that year she had wanted to go alone and he had discovered she was cheating again just as I had come on the scene. He had told her that he didn't want her back anymore and to stay away from the family home.

Four months into the relationship my son and I moved in with him and his daughter. When I first went round to the family apartment it was apparent that his wife had indeed just up and left for another man as all her belongings were still there. She had indeed left for a short trip and never come back, it seemed.[28]

The year we moved in with him was, I thought, blissful. The honeymoon period. While the children were away with their respective families, he and I would load up his van and have lovely, no-frills camping trips. He was glad to have a

---

27. An abuser will often form a relationship with another woman before the abusive relationship is over. A narcissist needs to be with his 'victim' in order to feel complete in himself. When a relationship is breaking down he will find himself a new victim. Or, while in a relationship where his partner is kicking back and not compliant, the narcissist will have an affair. He will come up with a million ways to explain it away if he is caught out.
This will include the continued 'blaming' of his ex. If that doesn't wash with you, he'll turn the tables and 'blame' you for not letting him explain properly, or for falling in love too quickly.
Whatever comes out of his mouth, it will not be him taking responsibility for any of it. He will frequently resort to the 'poor me' tactic.
28. In this scenario, it appears the ex-wife has left all her belongings behind. You have to ask yourself, 'why did she?'. It may be she didn't want them. Or, it may be, in the circumstances she was in, she had to leave quickly for her own safety.
We cannot know the truth in this situation, but at least remember that there are more sides to a story than his side.

woman who liked the simple things for a change. My son and I regularly visited my family back in England and in my mind that year was going to be no different. As usual, my mother and I started talking about our annual trip. We started organising and planning as my son got excited but that is when the questions started arising. Why would I want to go without him? Did I have someone else there?[19]

Why not wait and we can all go together? I suppose having your wife leave you all of a sudden would probably trigger some kind of jealousy, that was understandable, wasn't it? Being so jealous meant he loved and cared about me, didn't it?[29]

I was, as I've said in a good job, his daughter had never been to England so it was decided that that year the children would go alone and we would carry on working to save up to all go together. We never did.

Late one October night, about a year into the relationship, I got a call that woke us. My grandma had died. Although she had been unwell and an old lady the news was still upsetting. My grandma was close to all her grandchildren and was loved by all the family. I remember talking on the phone to one of my relatives in England and crying in bed. He woke up and in an angry voice told me to be quiet and to take the call elsewhere as he had to be up early for work.

---

29. *Jealousy. If someone's default position is thinking every time you are out of their sight, you are with another person/having sex elsewhere/being unfaithful, you must consider this as a deeply negative emotion. It is an indication that they are judging you by their standards.*
An abuser will judge everyone by their own beliefs and by the way they themselves would behave. In circumstances where an abuser will be unfaithful and blame the victim for the infidelity, then the abuser will believe that their victim will also think this way (it is ok to be unfaithful).

I was in shock by the news and his response and did as I was asked. The next morning, when I confronted him about his lack of sympathy and empathy, he looked hurt.[30]

He convinced me that he must have been sleep talking as he remembered nothing and that maybe, due to being upset, I may have taken things the wrong way and that he would never say anything like that intentionally.[22]

He was even upset that I would think that of him! Again I had an uneasy feeling in my gut that I brushed aside. There were to be many occasions like this in the years to come. It is called gaslighting and it is a dangerous, covert tactic commonly used by perpetrators. I would be taking things too seriously, couldn't take a joke or had misinterpreted or misunderstood him. On the odd occasion he would blatantly deny something he had done or said which would leave me feeling like I was going mad.

After two years we had our first child together and obviously life changed. It was decided that I would stay at home during the pregnancy and while the baby was small. During my first pregnancy I had taken maternity leave but the work I was doing at that time didn't offer that option. On the one hand, I was over the moon, as I was able to enjoy every moment, on the other, financially I was struggling.

The summer of 2006 I was heavily pregnant and it was decided that we would go with some of his family members, to an uncles house, who lived near the coast. The house was

---

30. Empathy (or lack of it). A narcissist will always put their own needs first. Rewind a year, to the 'honeymoon' period and all the talking and discussion. Where has that gone? That was 'grooming'.

in the middle of the countryside, a short drive away from the beach and boy, it was hot![30]

The plan was for all of us to be together, but it soon became apparent that his work commitments couldn't be avoided so he started leaving in the morning and coming back in the evening. As I didn't have a car and my sister-in-law didn't have space from my son and I, we were left at this isolated, sweltering house for a few days in a row. I remember feeling scared, lonely and very much put to one side.[19]

I asked if I could cut short my 'holiday' to which he insisted that he would be there in future and I was anxious over nothing.[31]

A month later our daughter was born. He was just the loving father I had expected him to be. The only problem was that he seemed to be spending more time at the bar with his friends. Money started to be an issue, the cleaner left and rent wasn't being paid.[32]

He told me that as his ex-wife didn't contribute towards

---

31. *Let's dissect this section.*
Very hot and isolated location. Heavily pregnant. No means of transport. The only option to leave her son behind. So, no means of transport.
Is this not an absolute pitch for a horror movie?? How frightening must this have been?
Horrible situation and devised entirely to isolate and dominate.
32. *Pregnancy/New birth. These High Risk indicators in DV murders.*
It is a very complex time in any relationship, but in an abusive one, it is a risk. It is also something that can happen early on in abusive relationships because it increases a woman's dependency and ultimately, connects people forever.
Taking no responsibility as a new parent in this case and going out with the boys. So the mother is literally left holding the baby, with all that comes with it, and his life hasn't changed at all.
Some men get jealous of the new addition to the family. This may seem crazy, but it happens. It is extremely dangerous for the child.

their daughter, it was her responsibility to pay the rent, but hadn't.[33]

My late grandmother had left me some cash which was used to clear the rent debts. Still money never seemed enough. My mother paid a visit to see her new grandchild and he sulked when we chatted on in English or went to the shops without him.[34]

Three months after my second child it was decided that to save money, we would move from the town centre to his parents' property in the country. It was a beautiful estate from the outside, plenty of land, with views of rolling hills, just perfect. His parents had the ground floor apartment and we occupied the small two bedroom apartment above. His daughter moved in with her other grandparents and my son and daughter would share a room. It was a new beginning and exciting times. I started working from home again giving English lessons to children and started making my own money again. He started hinting that all he needed now was a son.[35]

After just three months of having my second child I was expecting our third. I was over the moon to be starting my own little tribe.

---

33. Finances. There are articles that state worry over finances is a big cause for arguments. In this story, the perp still isn't taking responsibility for anything. Two years into this relationship, and he's still blaming his ex-wife for not paying the rent.

34. Sulking: I guess when someone speaks in another language, it can be difficult. Is it appropriate to point this out and say, 'that makes me feel excluded', or is it appropriate to sulk?

Sulking/the cold shoulder/ignoring. These are abusive behaviours. They are punishments.

Key to a healthy relationship is communication. If you don't say what the problem is, don't expect the other person to know what the problem is.

35. Some cultures value boys over girls. We see a disparity in some countries in boy/girl birth recordings. This is a massive subject and won't be covered in this book. However, if he wants a son, he is undervaluing you as a woman and any daughters.

My third child was born with an emergency C section. He was away working and wasn't there and I was scared. My new-born baby boy cried a lot but he would be spending more and more time at the bar, with his friends, after work. He would very often leave me with no money, no buggy, no keys or with some kind of excuse for me not to go out.[36]

My sister was visiting and we decided that I needed an evening out and he would 'babysit' the children. I don't remember much of what led up to it, but he wasn't happy that I was going out out. Push came to shove and I ended up being hit and with a black eye.[37]

I was heartbroken that he would do something like that and scared of what my future would look like as a single mother of three. After much crying he finally came home and apologised, much to my relief. I had pushed him to his limit, and I was to blame too. The next day his daughter helped me cover the bruise with make-up before I went out for a walk with the children. I bumped into a friend who noticed and told me he had done the same thing to his previous wife.[38]

The next few years weren't all bad as I tried my hardest to forget what happened and move on, but his behaviour got steadily worse.[39]

---

36. Trapped. No way of going anywhere. This is a way of excerpting power over you. He has the control. You have nothing.

37. Physical abuse. Under no circumstances is it ok to hit someone. Hitting someone is massively dangerous. There are no excuses for it. None. You did not 'push your luck', You did not 'wind him up'. You did not 'ask for it'. Physical abuse causes death. Run away!!

38. Why is it the people who 'know' always tell us afterwards? At this point, we are unpicking more of the story. If abusive behaviour is previously known, why don't people say it? Possibly because that person is still at risk and if the abuser is busy elsewhere, there's a logic behind that!

39.Escalation: Escalation is a High Risk factor in domestic violence murders. If things start cranking up in levels of violence and/or in levels of frequency, the alarm bells should ring.

He became the 'dominator', expecting me to behave, dress and express myself the way he suggested.[40]

He would withhold money, continually accuse me of cheating and spend more and more time at the bar with his friends. If I confronted him about his behaviour he would promise to change, promise marriage, promise the world and then, after a glimmer of respectful behaviour, I would see the evil streak come out in his eyes, I would see his fists clench and I would live like this for years.

After seven years together I fell pregnant with my fourth child. I had to leave the job I had recently started at a language school in the city. I cried when I found out. Shortly after giving birth money became even more of a problem and soon we began to lack essentials. That summer the water was cut off. I had four children under the age of eleven, in forty degrees heat, no running water and the situation soon became desperate. I decided to travel back to the UK with the children and stay with my mother until he found another place for us to live. This is when his paranoid behaviour really started to concern me as he was adamant that I had left him for somebody in the UK and would not reason with me about how essential water was! I spent hours on the phone convincing him that the issue was water and as soon as he had found us somewhere to live with water I would come back. He found a place in a town I didn't know, half an hour drive from the schools, right on top of a hill

40. *Dominator: This man uses a thousand different ways to abuse. He sulks, bullies, ignores, demands, the list goes on.*

surrounded by a few houses and countryside. The views were stunning in this small two bedroom house but things were about to get worse.[19]

The first seven years were a struggle. There were some very challenging times, but I was madly in love with him. He could be so charming and loving yet the more time he spent at the bar with his friend and with his father the worse he became. I couldn't understand why he couldn't be happy with me. I had already had children with two different men and the prospect of leaving him was not an option.[41]

He had always made it clear that, if for whatever reason, he wouldn't be allowed to see his children then neither would I.[42]

Looking back there were plenty of reasons for me to leave him, I should have left him, but I was blind. He convinced me that he wasn't that bad, he wasn't a wife beater as he had only hit me once but that was partly my own fault.[43]

---

41. *Self-esteem. Some women fear being left alone with children and that 'nobody will have me'. This is a mindset, and the mindset needs to be shifted.*
Picture this: Single mum of three meets new man. What if she said, 'It will be a privilege for you if I allow you into my life with me and my children. You need to up your game before that will happen'
An abusive partner will tell you nobody will want you so many times you will start to believe it! Hell, there are songs that tell you this...
'You'll never find, as long as you live..... Nobody loves you like I do....
Nobody's gonna love you like I do....
And on and on. No wonder women believe it! It is all BS! While we are on the subject of songs, I want to point out while some of them are good and catchy, all they do is maintain the pervasive idea that men are better than women, and women should be grateful for the attention. Of course, that's also BS!
42. *Threats about the children. This is setting off very loud alarm bells. There are cases of men taking their children and murdering them. Any perp who says, 'If I cannot, then you cannot' is a real and dangerous threat.*
43. *Only hit me once'. Well, that's ok then! NOT!! He is a violent abuser. The fact in this story is, he had to do it once to get the message across. After that, it was forever hanging in the air as a threat.*

He wasn't an addict, he rarely came back drunk, although he drank regularly.[44]

He went to work every day and provided what he could for his family. Ok, he had his mood swings and jealous paranoid behaviour but surely by showing him just how much I loved him, with time and patience, he would change, he promised.

"Are you wearing that to go out in?"

"Why so much make-up?"

"Watch what you get up to!"[40]

These were just some of the things he would say if I was going out without him. He wouldn't directly say no but there would be sulking or slamming every time I went out without him.

Living in that house on the hill made me even more isolated. One day I was sat at home when the finance police knocked the door. They explained that there were things that needed to be checked regarding his painting business. A few years earlier he had convinced me to put my name on his company due to some tax benefit for female business owners or something similar. I remember going with his mother to some offices with the small children in tow to sign some documents, but he had told me the job had subsequently fallen through and the plan had failed. This is not what the police were saying, and I had to go to the police station to

---

44. *Self-blaming. A perp will convince you it is all down to you. The narcissist cannot take responsibility for anything bad, ever. He will take credit for good stuff though.*
It does not matter what you do to try to resolve it. No amount of love, patience, self-denial, can fix a narcissist. You are not an expert in personality disorders (unless you are) and you cannot FIX IT. Don't try. You'll kill your soul, and he will let you.

make a statement. He told me not to worry as it was the accountant who had made a mistake, and everything would be fine. It wasn't. He didn't work in Italy again and we were forced to take up my mothers' offer and return to England .[45]

Unfortunately, my oldest son had important exams coming up and there was no space in the car for all of us so I had to leave him behind. This was the saddest day of my life.[46]

Once in the UK I was left to do everything, look for work, schools, housing, provide, work, cook, while he sat around and sulked. For six months until he joined us, I cried for my son. Once he told me it was my own fault for abandoning him, of course he was only joking! He didn't speak English and used this as an excuse for many years.[21]

For many years he continued to accuse me of having affairs and for many years I was holding on to his empty promises. One night it got so bad I was afraid he would strangle me, and I fled with the children to my mothers.[47]

She was a huge help at the time and couldn't imagine how I could cope without her. She then fell ill and was diagnosed with a terminal brain tumour. I was totally distraught, but his concerns lay in her new washing machine.[30]

---

45. Trust. What an awful situation. Easy to get sucked in to joint finances when you're in an intimate relationship and have children together.
As an aside, but on the same subject, in the UK, women have been sent to jail for non-payment of fines for not having a TV License! YES! INDEED! And who watches the TV??
46. Was this by design, I wonder? Separating a mother from her child is a form of torture and has been perpetrated for millennia!
47. Strangulation is a High Risk factor in domestic murders. It is difficult to strangle someone, and I cannot think of any other reason to put your hands around someone's neck.

Something snapped inside my gut, like a rubber band. I made a conscience decision to deal with my mother first and then him.[48]

In the meantime, we had booked a holiday to see his daughter. During this holiday I met his wife. They were not divorced. He had hit her, and she had left him due to his abuse, he had not owned any clothes shops as they were her parents, and he had not been to Taiwan.[49]

A year after my mother died, thirteen years after we had met, I left him. I was in debt due to his loans in my name, I had a note on my dbs. due to his corrupt business in Italy and I was alone with four children. It became the best decision of my life but life after a narcissist means things get worse before they get better.[50]

---

48. Snapping like an elastic band! This is exactly how I would describe the process when a victim leaves a perp.
Women leave, only to return. Like there's an invisible elastic band pulling them back. But, like an elastic band, every time it is stretched, it is slightly weakened. Until, one day, for whatever reason, that stretch causes the band to snap.
**** Please be aware, the HIGHEST RISK to your personal safety is when you make the decision to separate from your abuser.*
This book is written to help you avoid that abusive relationship entirely.
49. Lies and stories.
It is difficult to do a fact check on a new partner. It is sort of weird – in this time of social media, it is probably easier than it ever has been, but even so, Social Media is a front. Like a shop window. It is easy for anyone to look great on Facebook!
But if you uncover little lies, you'd better prepare yourself for bigger ones.
50. The end of a relationship is not always the end.

Affirmation

All I need is within me.

Story Two: Value yourself.

The author: The lady who wrote this story is a professional with numerous qualifications.

My first real job in a hospital aged maybe 18yrs shy and nervous but full of enthusiasm for my work and my life. Loved socialising with my now lifelong school friends, we were so close couldn't be closer, told each other everything. Enjoyed spending time with my work family, always laughing, making friends... life was easy.[1]

I have many memories of that time but one in particular I remember like yesterday. I was having a conversation with a nurse. A lady older than myself, she was a gentle and kind lady. I remember her one time chatting about her husband, she commented on him being a jealous type of person and I knew that she never really went anywhere. She never socialised outside of work with us, just her husband. I remember saying to her how it must be lovely to have someone like that, someone who loved her that much. I remember her glance at me and doing a half- hearted laugh but I didn't think anything of it and she seemed happy enough. I don't see that lady now, not for many years, but

---

1. As an observation, but generally, narcissists tend to attach themselves to people who are empathetic and caring. Someone who works to help others in a hospital based career would fit that profile.

I've chatted to her on social media and life seems good. But who knows?[2]

Looking back, I'm not quite sure why I admired her relationship so much. Did she appear to have her happy ending? Was it such a great feeling to have an all-consuming relationship was she so happy she didn't need friends or to socialise? I'm not saying this relationship was wrong for her, who am I to judge but I now know I had a skewed idea of what was appropriate in a relationship...probably my immaturity and lack of experience, after all I was 18.[3]

Fast forward to age 21. I was then single, my work colleagues enjoyed trying to match make so when a quiet student appeared on the ward, they chose the opportunity to try and work their magic and work it they did. We started going out on valentine's day. He charmed me with flowers and his quiet way seemed cute and harmless. It seemed to be

2. *The writer talks about a nurse colleague who has a jealous husband.*

- *This lady is also in a caring career.*
- *Jealous husbands/partners will do everything they can to isolate you from your friends and social life. And then they'll blame you for it! They'll accuse you of flirting, of having another boyfriend. They'll tell you your friends are bad people, and your friends are trying to spoil your relationship.*
- *Having someone care for you is lovely. Having someone obsessive and jealous is definitely NOT lovely.*

3. *Other people. What is right for one is wrong for another. No judging. Be open to letting people tell you when there is a problem.*

Something I'd like to drop in here:

"You've made your bed, now you have to lie in it" – Have you heard that before? Well, it is BS! I've often heard women saying it to other women. Their daughters. Their sisters!

And here's the pain: Women will collude with the abuse. In some cultures and religions, divorce is seriously frowned on and brings a stigma to the family. If this relates to you, please be very, very careful and seek help.

- *Karma Nirvana & Refuge.org*

These organisations will help.

However, it is nonsense to say that once you've chosen a relationship, and it is abusive, you have to stay. You don't. It is difficult to leave, and dangerous, but it is possible. This book is written to help you see the behaviours before you get involved with someone too closely.

a whirlwind romance, and everyone appeared happy for me. So when he 'suggested' we got engaged just weeks later I was excited...I was head over heels![4]

I knew there was issues in his family but he told me how he tried his best with them, but they had issues and problems, so they just weren't close. He lived with his grandma but that was only temporary as that often caused conflict and so he moved into bedsits. I felt for him as I came from a stable background with a loving family who I have to say weren't overly impressed at the speed of the engagement, but I told them how happy I was. All his personal issues stressed him, so I understood how anxious he was when I saw certain friends and when I wanted to go out with them, I always tried to give him lots of reassurance, sometimes it worked.[5]

He just seemed very insecure and made his opinions on my friends known and questioned why they were trying to come between us...I didn't think they were, but it became easier to just agree. I felt reassured that these were just teething problems and things would settle down.[6]

---

4. "A quiet student" – who knew?! Beware the wolf in sheep's clothing
Things moving fast. Proposal in just weeks at age 21.
Some people will say, "When you know, you know". This may be true for a minority, but a relationship is like a garden. You need to see it through the full cycle of seasons before you know what's in it.
5. Giving him lots of reassurance. Honesty and Trust are vital for the success of any partnership. If someone needs constant reassurance about where you are and who you are with, that's a concern. If you have not behaved in a way that would cause concern, think about why they are thinking this way. If they blame a previous partner, you need to put them straight. You should not be dealing with their baggage from something that is none of your business.
It is not your responsibility to deal with their past trauma. If there are unresolved issues, they should seek help.
6. To say your friends are trying to come between you is a classic act of the narcissist. He will do his best to isolate you from your friends and family.

Looking back, I wonder why I was unsure at times yet all I wanted was the typical first flush of love...it was there at times I'm sure.[7]

By the September of the same year, we were getting married. Again, my family couldn't understand the rush, but I said why wait...just as he'd said to me. It was tricky to plan things without my family's input...he thought it was better for us to plan it as it was our wedding, and I was so happy.[8]

Money was tight but the loan I got helped, he couldn't get one as he had one for his car. We had a house, our first home. I rented a dress because like I say money was tight. He had a lovely suit. I hated my dress but like he said, its only one day.[9]

The night before my wedding was exciting. I stayed home with my mam and sisters he went to the pub with his best man to-be. I have to say I had concerns, none that I'd said out loud but my gut was bugging me like an annoying little brother, poking me to get my attention. I ignored it...after all everything was paid for...booked. Did I really need my family to say told you so. No, fights and arguments were normal. Looking back, we were both so immature.[10]

---

7. *Being in love with being in love.*
We all feel this. We all want to feel loved and have butterflies! Give it time.
8. *"Why wait?". Someone who wants to control you will move as quickly as possible to get you into a situation where they can control you. Isolating you from your family is a big move, but common. They'll try to get you into a situation that's difficult to get out of, like getting pregnant or entering into a financial commitment.*
9. *Financial abuse.*
Take this scenario: He wants to get married FAST, but isn't taking financial responsibility for the wedding. But he does have a car, and a lovely outfit for The Big Day.
But her outfit isn't important. Already, her feelings aren't relevant. Can you hear the Sirens?!
10. *Gut feeling.*
Please, please, please, listen to your gut. It rarely gets things wrong. No matter how much money has been spent, arrangements made etc., it is NEVER too late to pull the plug. Pull the PLUG!!!!

I went home alone on my wedding night; I didn't mind he was enjoying himself.[11]

The first year of marriage was often not how I imagined it. The little niggles of getting to know you became big ones to the point we argued lots. He started going out a lot to the pub, sometimes not coming home till the next morning. He'd say he'd fallen asleep after playing cards. Of course this continued behaviour then resulted in arguments were I'd be told he'd stayed out because I was going on and on I found it very strange how he could say lots of hurtful things. Names I'd never been called before. They cant be unsaid. He was very argumentative which he seemed to enjoy.[12]

Don't get me wrong I wasn't perfect, but I did not 'enjoy' the rows.[13]

His behaviour was similar to his family's (mam, sisters, brother). They all had a very toxic relationship with each other. Bad language and cruel words were normality. It was alien to my family so when he spoke to my parents the same...

---

11. "I went home alone on my wedding night."
OMG! What?!! I so feel for this lady. Nobody, nobody, would think this is ok!
12. This is a guy who has positioned himself into a marriage but is not actually married in his behaviour. He's doing what he wants, when he wants. And then, because there are arguments, he 'blames' his wife for 'making' him want to stay out because she "goes on and on". Basic and standard abuse. It also seems he enjoys the arguing. Yes, because it gives him an excuse to continue with his selfish behaviour.
Being married or in an intimate relationship does not mean living in each other's pockets. But there is a need for balance and understanding.
13. "Don't get me wrong, I wasn't perfect".
Nobody is. Reflecting behaviour back onto themselves is a common reaction from DV victims.
Just get this clear – you ARE allowed to be angry, to argue and to fight back when you are being abused.
It is a basic right! It doesn't put you into the category of Abuser, or "giving as good as I get", because you're NOT!

We were shocked. Where was the respect! That is one of my worst regrets, allowing them to be spoken to like that.[14]

I remember the day that it came to a head. My close friends knew that things weren't quite right and that I'd moved into the spare room. I was stubborn and if he wanted to separate... well why should I leave! One day my parents had left my house after he'd been vile to them. I defended them and encouraged them to leave. I just wanted to protect them.[15]

As they drove away, he turned to me said 'wave goodbye to mammy and daddy' and then dragged me off the sofa by my legs, scraping my back over the sofa and across the floor. As my back grazed along the carpet, he told me how this was all mine and my parents' fault. He crouched down, spat venom in my face, made some threats and left me laid there and he left the house. It was the first time id actually been scared of him. I packed my things and left him. I'd had enough but...I still loved him. You cannot just flick a switch and turn your feelings off.[16]

---

14. *All families have their own 'ways'. If your family is very different from your boyfriends, please look at that, especially, like in this scenario, where the lady is shocked by how his family behave.*
It is not about money, or how big the house is, education or religion. It is about basic manners and how we behave towards each other.
15. *He's isolated her from her parents and then assaults her– then blames her and her parents. Again, a narcissist will never take responsibility. Never.*
16. *Love – "you cannot flick a switch". No, you cannot, but you can realize this is not the love you are looking for.*
Definition of Love from the Oxford Dictionary:
An intense feeling of romantic attachment based on an attraction felt by one person for another; intense liking and concern for another person, typically combined with sexual passion.
Therefore, he cannot love you (or anyone) and never will, regardless of what he says.
It is OK that someone doesn't love you. It is not YOU, it is them. You are a lovable person with many wonderful things coming your way. If someone doesn't love you, that's ok. Someone else will. Love yourself first! Do not get confused between love and attachment. They are different things

I'd married for love and he...I think looking back, initially I was a roof over his head. Some sort of meal ticket.[17]

A couple of days later I saw him hand in hand with another girl.[18]

This then all made sense why he'd been going out, not coming home etc.

They both got a shock when I appeared in front of them. She claimed he'd told her we were separated but way longer than a few days. He stood there in shock. I probably shouldn't have done this, but I punched him right across his face. My sister took me back to the car. How humiliating. I was broken hearted.

Long story short, he spent the next few weeks convincing me of his mistakes that were nothing more than that and nothing had happened (sex) and how much he loved me, even got his sisters on board. All I could see around me was everyone with their happy ending and all I wanted was mine. Was that too much to ask for?

So, after listening to his tears and begging. I cancelled the solicitor and against my family's wishes, went back.

Aha! the thing that would repair any damage would be a baby we thought. We didn't consciously say that, but I think

---

17. A narcissist is a person who will take advantage of another persons' kind heart. In this case, the perp has used the victim to find himself a home and someone to pay for him, while he takes no responsibility.

18. Infidelity. Normal for an abuser. He doesn't respect you and will do whatever he wants to do. He'll even blame you for his infidelity by saying things like...

"If you hadn't done...." "If you were more..."

"You made me do it because you...." etc.

It is inevitable an abuser will shift every ounce of responsibility onto anyone but themselves.

we thought it. After all I'd so wanted to be a mam, I knew how much I'd love it. I was 23...women planned their families young in those days. Now 23 is barely an adult.[19]

The time went by, his moods would be really up or really down... black. I encouraged him to get some counselling, which he did. He stopped after no time at all, didn't work 'load of rubbish'[20]

The poisonous words continued; it broke my heart when he would say them in front of my child. I just didn't understand why. Nothing seemed to start his behaviour, it just was.[21]

He always had a reason why, me usually and sometimes after my reaction, he'd apologise.[22]

---

19. Babies. Will a baby help? Probably not.
Having a baby is stressful, tiring, expensive, physically draining and probably the most difficult and challenging thing in any relationship. So why have one when the relationship is struggling?
And age makes no difference. 23 or 43, the same principles apply.
And once you have a baby, a baby is forever. It ties you to the other parent.
20. Making an effort. An abuser will listen and take on board what you say. Then they will use that information against you and tie you in knots. An abuser has no intention of changing their behaviour. Why would they? There are no consequences. They'll take things in and then dismiss them, even the top professionals, as "rubbish". Then, down the line, they'll say, "well, I tried, but it didn't work for me". They didn't try. They pretended to try.
21. DV and children. If you are in an abusive relationship and there are children, your children are in an abusive relationship. And they have no choice!
22.Triggers. Some will say you "push their buttons" and their behaviour is down to you. This is nonsense. They behave as they do because they choose to.
Take this as an example:
A man goes out with his mates for a few drinks in town. Coming home, he gets a bus, pays his fare to the driver and sits down in a seat. He might chat to one or two other passengers. Maybe he's a little tipsy, that's fine.
He gets off at his stop and walks the 300 yards to his home. On the way, he says "good night" to a couple of people passing.
He meets his neighbour at the gate and has a chat.
He opens the door with his key and locks the door carefully.
He goes into the front room and his wife says, "you said you'd be back before 10" and he punches her.
The neighbour hears the screaming and calls the police. The man is arrested.
During the police interview, he tells the officer, "She knows how to push my buttons. I lost control".
Did he lose control?
Why did he 'choose' to lose control at that point? He didn't. He was very much in control.
DV is about Power and Control.

He would go from poisonous to Mr Charming day to day, hour to hour even. He loved me one minute the next I was a stupid c*** . It was hard to know if I'd wake up with Dr Jekyll or Mr Hyde. Believe me that is a horrible gut-churning feeling.[23]

I often wonder now, if he did it in front of the children to hurt me. Knowing how I couldn't bear to hear him say those things and even more for them to hear it. It was harder to hide it from my eldest child as he was attached to my side always. We did everything together and I do think at times my husband felt left out. It is hard to involve him when he didn't want to be involved. Laying on sofa was always his preferred choice.[24]

When the next two children came along it was the same. However, they enjoyed the Xbox with earphones (thankfully). So, in later years it was easier for me to hide their dad's behaviour as they would be in their rooms oblivious, I'd hoped.[25]

I would manage to clean up any plates of food he'd thrown or items he'd broke before they came downstairs. Protecting my children became my purpose and rightly so but, along the way I suppose I wrongly forgot my worth and stopped protecting myself.[26]

---

23. *Mood swings. Mr Nice -v- Mr Nasty.*
What a great way to keep you on your toes! You walk on eggshells because you don't know who he is today. That's Control.
24. *Being jealous of his own children. Putting things in place to spoil the day deliberately. A typical abusive behaviour. His choice but blaming everyone else.*
25. *Earphones or not, it is impossible to hide abuse from children. They are resilient and know when to get out of there. Child abuse is part of Domestic Abuse, and there is no splitting it.*
Small children get hurt because they cannot get out of the way!
26. *At this point the storyteller is at her lowest. No self-worth. All her energy going into protecting her children from their father. Imagine that. That feeling of exhaustion but having to keep going!*

The years went by and it continued. I often thought of leaving, I used to look in the local paper for flats to rent. How would I manage though, with three children and not a lot of money? I worked but only part time.[27]

I was exhausted bringing up three children doing all the housework and cooking and still working. If I asked him to help, he would reply well if you can fix the boiler when it breaks than I'll get the hoover out! As if that was going to happen![28]

My mum knew. I never said, never told her things he said and did. She just knew. They'd go on holiday and she'd say, 'Now you have a key to come home if you need to'. That's it.

I never went home, I never told them. I had my reasons.[29] When my third child was one, my mum got diagnosed with terminal lung cancer. Me, my sister, and my dad spent around six months looking after her between home and hospice. It was devastating. I always had to take my baby with me. I remember coming home from the hospice one day (with

---

27. *Dreaming about another life probably saved this lady's sanity. Many women are stuck in abusive relationships because they simply cannot afford to leave. Apart from taking part time work after having children, many partners are financially co- dependent. Maybe it is school fees that cannot be paid and the children would have to change school. Maybe it is basics like earning enough to rent a small property.*

28. *His chores –v- Her chores.*

Does this sound familiar? Girls do housework. Boys fix cars. Really?! Learn how to change a plug and a car wheel. For everything else, you can pay an expert to do it.

If a man isn't prepared to take some of the burden of household upkeep, he's no thought for you having to do it. Someone has to clean the toilet!

Read this article www.harpersbazaar.com/culture/features/ a12063822/emotional-labour-gender-equality/

29. *Bless her mum! Trying to give her an escape route. But it is so difficult. If you know someone who is in an abuse relationship, never give up trying to help.*

When you ask someone, "How are you?", ask them three times. Most people reply "I'm fine" even when they aren't. So, ask again, "What's happening in your world?". Give them a chance to open up. If they still say they're fine, ask "Tell me about what's fine then."

the baby) he was cutting the grass. I asked him where my middle child was, he would have been home from nursery about twenty minutes previously. My husband stated, 'nursery probably'. When I asked why he had not been and collected him his words were 'NMP' this was a term he used probably on a daily basis if he deemed something was 'not my problem'. I truly could not believe that he had left our child at school on purpose. I quickly rang school, made an excuse, and ran to get him. Shocking. He had been off work doing nothing at all except cut the grass which would have taken 30 mins tops.[30]

He obviously hated the lack of attention he was getting as my mum was my focus, as she should be. When we planned her funeral just a few weeks later, my husband was furious that I wanted to travel in the hearse with my dad, brother, and sisters. Our partners would come in their own cars and sit in row behind us in the chapel. We, as his children, would support our elderly father.[31]

He made me feel so guilty for leaving him out. Me and my sister spoke about it...me giving the sympathy vote to my husband under pressure. I feel so bad about that. She told me to do whatever I needed to. I wish I could tell her everything now. Arrangements got changed slightly to cater for him and he even made his opinion known what announcements

---

30. A narcissist is relentless in their abuse. They will take any scenario and use it to abuse. They don't care how bad it is. They simply don't care. You cannot change that. Don't even try. Millions have gone before you and failed because this is not failing. You cannot fail if you are attempting the impossible.
31. Making excuses for the abuser's behaviour. This is a form of self-protection. A victim will squirm with embarrassment at the thought of anyone challenging his behaviour because, regardless, it puts even more pressure on her.
This is something people struggle to understand.

needed to be in the paper. I'm so annoyed with myself and I cannot turn back the clock oh how I would.[32]

Whilst my mam was poorly, my sister had been going through her own tragedy of breast cancer. We were so close, and I did everything I could to help support her and her family whilst my own heart broke. How would I cope with no mam and no sister?

Apart from my kids they were my only safe haven and I loved them so much.

There were times when my husband was a good support then. It was only short lived and to be honest, I now think it was fake...all show for those who could see. If only they'd knew the real him.[33]

Lots of people understand domestic violence to be physical, not always.

Yes, I've had things thrown at me enough to bruise and leave a mark but never a fist.

I've been held down by my wrists and spat at in my face but never a punch.

I've been threatened if I moved out and take my children then they'll have nothing, and I'll have nothing to give them but never a slap.

When you're told so many times that other people's relationships are just like this and they just don't tell you... you begin to believe it.

---

32. *Self-righteous and privilege. How shameful for her, and of him. But he doesn't care as long as he gets his own way. He hasn't got the capacity to care.*
33. *Faking it. Many relationships look good on the surface, when really, it is a sham. He wants others to think he's the perfect partner. The acting in public comes naturally. It is a show.*

The shame stops you asking others ... is it normal?[34]

When you look around and hope that tomorrow will be a better day then there's a chance you might get that happy ever after.

I look back now and I see so many behaviours that were irrational, aggressive, harmful. but at the time I swallowed the nausea and did what I had to do. My dad now needed me...again others came first. I made excuses to dad if there was a mark. I made excuses why my husband wouldn't come to family gatherings or why I didn't go. I made excuses why I couldn't go out or if I did, why I couldn't eat certain foods... the list goes on.[35]

You might be thinking foods? It is surprising a reaction you can get by going out for a meal with friends....shouted at for smelling of garlic, kicked and I mean kicked out of bed to sleep on sofa or in spare room. Punished.[36]

I know he was jealous that I had friends...he would try his best for years to get me to not see them, but I would never give up my dear friends. Some friends I lost touch with and others... it is easier to keep your distance from as then its less people to lie to (sorry) some friends you cannot live without (you know who you are). I didn't go out often at all but when

---

34. *Domestic violence IS; .having things thrown at you; .being held down; being spat on; being threatened; being fooled and being shamed*

35. *Hiding it from others. Women do this, not just to protect themselves, but to protect others. Remember, victims are targeted because they are caring people.*
They care for people and want to protect them. They make excuses because they are embarrassed. If we are more open about DV, and challenge abusive behaviours right from the beginning, we wouldn't have this embarrassment. The embarrassment would fall to the abuser. Call him out. Don't let him get away with it

36. *The food is just an excuse to mete out the punishment. You go out without him, expect to be punished.*

I did it cost me heavily. We had to have sex before I went out then he'd phone/text me all night.[37]

One night I'd not had a signal so when I came home he was gone.[38]

He'd left kids in house alone, to drive around pubs to 'catch me out'.[39]

Oh, by the way, I was always having affairs, flirting, being generally devious! In his eyes. He went ballistic on his return, as you can imagine how the usual cold shoulder for days played out. He was always the victim.[40]

The kids never wanted me to go to work or for a night out. I thought that was normal as they were used to me being with them all the time. I got the impression they just went to their rooms when I wasn't home.[41]

As time went on, the situation began to play on my health. I didn't realise at the time, I thought I was just run down,

---

37. Using his cock as a power tool. This is a man who is raping his wife to mark his territory. "We had to have sex!" = he raped me.
Please notice how the writer has skimmed over this as "normal". Because, for her, it is normal. Rape is rape.
Statistically you are more likely to be raped at home than anywhere else. Stranger rape does happen. One reason stranger rape is so horrific – the victim doesn't know they don't know the rapist
38. Constant calls and texts. This covers a couple of things: It spoils her night and he's checking up on her location
39. Complete lack of care for his children. He is obsessed by his imaginings of her non-existent infidelity. It is all in his head. It is all his standard. Right from the beginning, he was the one who was unfaithful. He is setting his standard to her behaviour, and she can do nothing about it. He accuses her of infidelity. It is not real. He knows that. But he'll do it anyway.
40. The cold shoulder. Withdrawing affection is abusive. Being moody is abusive.
Here's another example.
Bedtime. You have an intimate relationship. You like to have sex. He has a hard on, but instead of loving you, he turns away. How do you feel? Rejected? Unloved? Unlovely? That's deliberate. That's emotional abuse.
41. The children are aware of the abuse. They know what the consequences are for them and their mum.

stressed. As health issues played out his irrational behaviour continued. He would phone ward constantly at times....I mean every few minutes. It was embarrassing having to make stuff up.[42]

I think when I was leaving the ward, he saw it as his chance to have me at home 24/7 but I moved departments as I didn't want to just be at home. His dream was us moving away. Somewhere remote just us once kids had left home. The thought filled me with dread.[43]

In between night shifts and looking after my dad and the kids I decided to retrain. Working with children was something I'd often thought about but he would put me off by saying how those jobs were too hard to get, I'd never get one.[44]

Against him I took myself to a part time course. I had to pay but tell him it was free.[45]

I wasn't really allowed to buy things without his say so.

I often found myself secretly buying things but silly insignificant things that shouldn't matter, like make up. He

---

42. *The emotional strain in an abusive relationship is immense. Women are prescribed anti depressants to help them cope. Basically, it is not depression (or maybe it is). It can be cured by removing the abuser from the equation.*

43. *His dream is moving away".*
Isolation is a HIGH RISK factor in DV homicides. Both physical isolation – moving away from your support network of friends and family, and emotional isolation – working to get to a situation where friends and family start to avoid coming round or working to prevent any socializing.

44. *Undermining confidence. Repeatedly telling her she's no good, incapable, less able.*
Women have their self-esteem eroded.
The abuser doesn't want their prey to be "better" than them, whatever "better" means in their head. It clashes with their ego and inflated sense of importance.

45. *Finances. Financial abuse is common. Holding the money is holding the ability of someone to live their life. Checking on spending, shopping receipts, is a way to control someone.*

hated me wearing make up, so he would've gone mad me wasting money on it.[46]

I was enjoying my course, he said I was selfish.[47]

I completed a second course then I got myself a new job.

The relationship continued but his behaviour became more irrational.[48]

He started tracking me on my phone, I continued to make excuses why things got broken in house, doors...walls etc.[49]

I continued being some sort of go between with him and the neighbours. He hated them all, he said they were trying to damage his car so he put up CCTV. The neighbours were lovely, I struggled to see issues.[50]

He went on from Mr Happy one day to wishing he had cancer in order to get some sympathy, the next.[51]

---

46. Make-up. Slut Shaming. Making you feel like you shouldn't wear makeup is common.
"You don't need it" "You're pretty enough" You look like a hooker"
"who are you trying to impress?" You cannot win.
Wear makeup for yourself if you want to. Don't dress for anyone but yourself. We all like to look and feel good. Feel good for you.
47. Doing things for yourself will be labelled 'selfish'. Doing the normal things, that everyone does. Self-care is not selfish, it is essential.
48. "his behaviour became more irrational"
Know this – unless there's some intervention, things get worse, not better. He will 'crank up' his behaviour to hurt you more. He will not change.
49. Stalking is a HIGH RISK factor in DV homicides. People can be, and are, stalked by their current partners as well as ex partners. He will keep an eye on what you are doing. Secretly follow you. Track your phone.
50. Making excuses for him is a defence mechanism. Please be aware a victim will defend her abuser. It is a form of self- preservation.
I have arrested an offender and his victim has 'kicked off' and screamed for him not to be arrested. On the face of it, it seems crazy, but it isn't. She knows he is likely going to continue his abuse, regardless of the outcome of the arrest and any court order. At least, if she does this, he sees he's got her onside and he's less likely to give her another kicking when he gets home. It is horrible.
51. Attention seeking is normal for a narc. He will take you on his rollercoaster ride. Threats of suicide are normal but be aware, someone who is suicidal should also be regarded as homicidal.

To taking us out for the day (only ever where he wanted to go) to telling me to get house in order as he was gonna kill himself. My health suffered again...I now believe it was all stress related.[52]

One time I was so ill I asked him to phone and they sent an ambulance. I couldn't even get peace then, he was aggressive to ambulance staff and slammed door behind us as we got into ambulance. I was so embarrassed and apologised to them.

I think I must have been in some sort of fog to allow this to continue, I just don't know.[53]

He had a habit of embarrassing me, he must have enjoyed it. Whether it was on a very, very rare night we went out or on the phone. I remember once being on the phone to the car insurance company and for no reason he laid there on sofa with aggressive body language just berating me for nothing. Calling me names, swearing, revving himself up. I cried silently with my back to him as the man on the other end of the phone said 'pet I'm going to turn off my headset for you, you don't need the humiliation of me hearing that, I'm sorry.'[54]

I could have fell into a hole and died, I was beyond mortified.

---

52. *Anything that takes attention away from him will be punished. In this case, he's deliberately embarrassing her.*
53. *This is so sad, the victim is blaming herself. We do not allow bad behaviour. It is not our responsibility how adults behave. It is their choice.*
54. *The perp does enjoy inflicting pain. It is what they live for. They will shame you publicly at every opportunity.*

It was my birthday, we went out to an event. We walks up to the bar, orders a drink. Apparently, the way I asked him, showed him up. He stormed off for about an hour. Left me stranded miles away from home and no transport. I sat in there on my own till he came back, he didn't speak but at least I could now get home. Happy birthday to me.

The day I left his behaviour had gone off the chart all week and I couldn't bear it no more...he threatened me all day by text/ calls/emails so when the kids came home from school we left.[55]

This is one of the things I do not regret.

It is been five years now...long, long divorce but not as long as the 23yrs of mostly unhappiness. He tried to promise me the world if I went back...never. He promised me holidays... was he joking, every holiday with him had been awful for me ...it was different surroundings, same pain.

Some scars go deep, the nightmares still come and I wish I could wipe some memories away however...now life is hard but happier...my house is smaller but a home...I know I can tell my friends anything and the kids make me, nothing else, they were worth it.

---

55. *The final straw! Please remember, some people never get to the point where they leave. Remember the nurse colleague at the beginning?*
The writer doesn't say why this was her Moment. It could be something big or something small.
The bombardment of threats by all systems is HIGH risk. This is Escalation.
This is after 23 years with this man.
The perp will beg and plead. Their promises are false. They are liars. They will not change unless events happen that force them to change.

Affirmation

My thoughts have power.

Affirmation

I can take a bad day and turn it into a good day.

Story Three: There is No Need for Speed

The author: The lady who wrote this story is now a businesswoman

I was 17 when I met my future husband, he was 22, I met him in the February, engaged in the May, on my 18th birthday, and married in the October. Little did I know that that's what narcissistic people do, they get them young and condition them to how they want.[1]

I became pregnant very quickly,[2] his idea, although I'd always wanted children. When I was eight months pregnant with my first child, I woke up one morning to my husband tying my feet to the bed.

I was completely shocked,[3] I had just turned 19, didn't have a clue what was happening. I asked him what on earth was he doing, that's when I first seen the darkness that I was going to become very familiar with. He still had my leg in his hand and just threw it to the bed.

---

1. Be careful about hurrying. This lady was married in under a year.
When we meet a new partner, we have amazing emotions and we are "in love". Feelings of euphoria and "butterflies". This is lovely but give it a while. Don't get railroaded into marriage, living together or pregnancy.
Which leads me to...
2. Getting pregnant is a wonderful thing. A time for celebration. But just make sure that the time is right for you. Take your time. Don't get pregnant to fill a hole in your life.
3. There are a couple of things here. Tying someone to the bed when they are asleep is massively dangerous behaviour.
And there's S&M. Some people like being tied up for sexual pleasure. The people involved must consent!

Soon after I gave birth to my beautiful little boy, never had I felt love like that before. When my son was three months old, I became very poorly, gastric flu, never been that ill, before, or since. My husband completely ignored my pleas for, fluid, help or a doctor.[4]

I think he became quite scared when I was drifting in and out of consciousness, because he eventually called a doctor out to me. I was in bed and only got half of the conversation because I was drifting, I heard the doctor ask how long I'd been like that for, didn't hear my husband's reply, but I knew the doctor really wasn't happy. I don't know how long I was there for, before or after to be honest.[5]

After my son was born sex went downhill, it was just so painful, didn't know till six years later when I was three months pregnant with my second child, that the midwife who had performed the stitches had stitched me up like a Cornish pasty (the words of the surgeon when he told me). Didn't make any difference to my husband, he owned me, so he had a right to have me whenever he wanted, painful or not.[6]

I went through 19 years of hell, didn't realise my children

4. No empathy. It is difficult to understand when a person appears not to care about someone who is their partner and lets them suffer. Something to remember...a narcissist doesn't have empathy. The world is all about them. Empathy is what they lack.
You cannot fix this in a narcissistic person.
5. Safeguarding. When anyone in authority comes into contact with a person who they believe to be at risk, there is now a process in place for them to make sure that person gets help. This is relevant when children are involved.
6. Nobody has a right to force you to have sex. That is rape. If you find sex painful, speak to your doctor. Abusive people believe that have a "right" to you. Physically, emotionally, sexually. They don't. Your body is yours.
Your vagina and your virginity belong to you.

had as well, and that breaks my heart more than anything else, especially my eldest, because he'd blamed him for the fact that I didn't want sex.[7, 8]

He'd wake me up three, four times a night for sex, sometimes I'd wake up and he'd already trying to have sex with me.[9]

I spent years of lying rigid on the end of the bed in fear of moving in case he woke up because he'd want sex, even after 17 years of not being with him I still wake up to find myself on the edge of the bed.

I went through years of emotional and physical abuse, I was told what to wear,[10] who I could see and he constantly checking up on me, for instance, he'd call my mobile, ask where I was, I'd tell him I was home and he'd phone the landline, just to make sure I was there.[11, 12]

If he didn't get his own way, he would sulk for weeks on end, making my children's life and mine a complete misery. I couldn't turn the heating on, if me and my children were sat on the sofa together watching TV and he walked in from work we'd get "what the fuck are you watching this for" and

---

7. If there is abuse in a relationship, then this is also child abuse.
The children don't have to be in the same room, building, or even town!

8. The abuser used this ridiculous reason to put more abuse onto the victim. He feels he has a right to do this. He thinks he is the centre of the world.

9. Sexual abuse. In this story, regardless of the situation, this behaviour is a High Risk behaviour. Forcing someone to have sex constantly is high risk. In this case, he's also including some sleep deprivation. Sleep deprivation is used as a form of torture.

10. The Dominator. Dictating everything. The Bully. He sees himself as the king of this particular castle.

11. Constantly checking up. Cross checking. Cross examining. An abuser uses their values as a yardstick for everyone else. They believe others are capable of the things they themselves would do. It is difficult to live life when your abuser is setting themselves as a standard.

12. Sulking is a form of abuse. It is childish and solves no problems. But an abuser does not want to solve problems they don't see as problems.

he'd turn it off, then I'd know I was in for a bad night.[10]

Many times he'd have me up against the wall by my throat with his fist in my face,[13] threatening to punch me if I didn't do what he asked, or degrading me by calling me fat,[14] or saying would have you, look at the state of you now, who'd want you with five kids, where would you go, all your family are dead. I never knew until much later that there was such a thing as a woman's refuge.[15]

After I gave birth to my child,[5] I had major surgery on my stomach, I was in hospital for four days and when I was sent home I was told, no driving, ironing, housework or heavy lifting for six weeks, I told my husband and when I got home I had friends coming to visit, my husband was in the middle of fitting a new kitchen, which had taken him several months, and there plaster board and dust everywhere. I asked if he would at least hoover up because I was so embarrassed by the mess, and he said "no because I wasn't giving it up" meaning sex.[16]

When my youngest was two or three weeks old I got a womb infection, I was so poorly I couldn't get off the sofa,

---

13. *Grabbing someone by their throat is HIGH RISK behaviour. There is no reason to grab someone's throat other than to strangle them.*
14. *Physical violence is a HIGH RISK behaviour. Any assault can turn into serious injury or death.*
15. *Insults are intended to erode your confidence. This takes us to look at how we perceive ourselves and how we think we are perceived by others. I've heard women say, "Who would want me? I've got x number of children" or "I don't think anyone else would be interested in me".*
This is because when we are told something enough times, we start to believe it. Confidence is eroded. When we have babies, our bodies change. In this western culture, the media portrays slim as desirable. Slimming and being slender are seen as desirable. (When I typed that sentence, the auto-corrector wanted me to change it to "Slimming and being slender are desirable" – that's how entrenched this is! WOW!)
What if we exercised to be strong instead of to be skinny?
16. *Who to go to for help? There is a list of organizations for in the UK at the back of this book -* *see page 107*

he just walked out and left me lying on the sofa. Luckily, a friend came to visit and took me to the doctors.[4]

Then at the beginning of February 2003, he'd gone out for a drink with his friend, he got home, I was already asleep in bed,[17] he got into bed and started to try and have sex with me. I woke up and told him no, he jumped out of bed and pulled the quilt off me, threw a bottle of beer over me and held me down by my throat. This time he walked out and left for seven days, in between that week my brother, who was an alcoholic, was rushed to hospital where he went into a liver coma, it was touch and go and we thought he was going to die. My husband used that vulnerability and used it to his advantage to take him back, which of course I did. I told him that if he ever lay a hand on me again, I would divorce him. My brother made a full recovery but passed away 10 months later.

Things went okay until the 3rd March 2003, again he'd been out with his friend, I'd been for food with mine, I was in bed when he got home. He started to try and have sex with me, I said no, and he got very violent quickly. He jumped out of bed, dragged me out, got me up against the dressing table, held me by my throat and head butted me, threw me out the door and down the stairs. My eldest who was 18 at the time, asked him why he was doing what he was doing. [18] He let go of me and started attacking my son, had him on the

---

17. Using vulnerability to get his own way. We all have periods of vulnerability. Remember, at this stage, the lady is years into the relationship. She's suffering the isolation because her abuser has made this so. He is likely the only adult she has regular contact with.

18. Humiliating the victim in front of their children is child abuse.

sofa punching him in the face, calling him a little bastard. I tried to stop him, and he got hold of me, threw me out of the door and shut it. Thankfully, I had my mobile, so I called the police, minutes later my husband then threw my son out, all his face was bloody, completely destroyed me.

We went over to my friends while we waited for the police, I'd informed the police that my youngest[4] was still in the house with him and I was really concerned. The police arrived about 45 minutes later.

My husband was arrested[19] and charged, my statement was taken but as it was taken in front of my son I couldn't tell him the beating was because I'd said no to sex. They asked my son for a statement and he said he couldn't,[20] I think that's when I realised there was more to why he'd refused. The policeman said they have the power to charge his dad without his statement.

My husband got out three days later, instantly my phone started to ring, both landline and mobile, I knew it was him because I'd already had a call from the domestic abuse unit. He emptied the bank, I couldn't get food unless he got it for me, didn't make any difference that he had bail conditions on him,[21] he couldn't come near me or the children. The

---

19. Being the Big Man of the house. Sometimes, the Lion King feels threatened by the lion cub and excerpts his dominance by using physical violence on a child. We see this in the world of apes and mammals. Many times, this is the moment when, after years of abuse, a mother will have a moment of 'now or never' and leave the relationship. A dangerous time.

20. Giving a statement to the police will now normally be in private and recorded on video rather than on paper.

There are now Special Measures to help witnesses give evidence in court.

21. It is difficult for a child to put in a complaint against a parent or significant adult. After years of fear and humiliation, it must be terrifying.

phone calls and the threats continued, I'd get flowers one day then the police the next because my husband had said I'd left the children in on their own. I hadn't it was the only way he could get at me.[22]

Six weeks after I received a phone call on my landline one Sunday, I picked it up, and thank goodness it was me; it was a man asking for my services. My husband was seen in a local shopping centre handing cards out, on this card was my landline number, my body measurements on it, and that I liked it doggy style. I explained my situation to the man on the phone, told him that his sexual preferences haven't got anything to do with me, but could I have that card. I told him I had children and that anyone of them could've picked the phone up. I went with a friend to pick it up, he owned a pub which is where I picked it up from.[23, 24]

In June of that year it was my daughter's birthday, I'd bought her presents, not a lot because I didn't have any money, my husband had made sure of that. I was putting her presents on top of my wardrobe in my bedroom and I found

---

22. *Authority. It is usual practice, if a person is on police or court bail, for bail to have conditions attached to it, for example: they might be told not to contact the victim by any means, or be told where they must live until everything is sorted out. If the person ignores the conditions, it is evidence they have no respect for authority. They believe they are above the law. This person is extremely dangerous.*
23. *Maximum disruption. When the abuser loses the control he has over the victim, he will try to use other ways to continue the abuse.*
In this example he's called the police to say the children have been left alone. Of course, the police are obliged to check the story, even though they are aware of the history.
This is an example of where an abuser uses the authorities to continue the abuse.
Ringing Social Services is also a common tactic.
24. *Annihilating someone's character. These days it is usually social media where lies are posted. Be careful on social media.*
25. *Placing a CCTV camera in the house can be for several reasons. It is to keep watch on what the occupants are doing. Remember the abuser was always accusing his victim of infidelity? It looks like he was checking up on this.*

a CCTV camera[25] that the wire was going towards the attic. I didn't have any idea how long that had been there.

My husband continued with his manipulation by trying to get my son to take him back.[26] My son was going on his first holiday with his friends, and his dad told him he could do some work with him and he'd give him money to spend on his holiday. My son worked for two weeks and at the end his dad said he'd give him the money if he got me to take him back. So I sold all his tools from the shed and gave the money to my son.

October, it went to court,I was made to feel like the criminal, I was made to feel like it was all my fault, he was allowed to change his statements several times, one being he hit me because his tea wasn't on the table. He was made to pay me.[27]

£100 compensation and my son £150 and was given 180 hours community service.

After a threat from him when he threatened to slit my throat,[28] the domestic abuse unit put me and the children

26. *Using the children. Children just want people to be nice to them and to others. When an adult makes promises, children believe it.*
27. *Criminal proceedings in the UK:*
The defendant is presumed innocent until proven guilty. The defence solicitor is there to do a job for their client. Many offenders will deliberately employ a female solicitor. They think that people will think "He cannot be an abuser, his brief is female. Surely a woman wouldn't defend a domestic abuser" It is a strategy. Giving evidence in court can be very daunting. They try to trip you up and get you to change your story. They try to discredit you. It is part of the process, but almost impossible not to take it personally.
28. *Relentless and ongoing. Because a relationship ends, does not mean the abuse ends. One thing you need to realize (and probably why I've written this book) is, when you get involved with an abuser, it is very difficult to get uninvolved with them.*

in a woman's refuge in south wales, my eldest wasn't allowed because he was 19, they helped him get a flat.[29] Still my husband would manage to find my mobile number and phone me with threats.

He then started to fight for access to the children,[30] my eldest was back living with me then as I'd got a house in Cardiff. CAFCAS got involved and came and got statements from the children. My eldest was 21 at this point and asked if he could give a statement, my son was told he could if he wanted to, but he doesn't have to because of his age, my son said he wanted to because he didn't want his brother and sisters to go through what he went through. My eldest went in and made a statement, after the statement he came into the kitchen to me and my partner, and said "mum I need to tell you something now because it is going to come out now anyway" my stomach dropped, all thoughts were going through my head. My son, after what felt like a lifetime, eventually continued to tell me that when he was six or seven, he was playing with a plug socket, and his dad electrocuted him to teach him that if he continued then that's what will happen, I was devastated, completely and utterly heartbroken. I asked where I was and he said I was

---

29. *Refuges do amazing work. However, teenage boys are rarely allowed to stay. This is because the residents have had negative experiences with men. It is also heart breaking to not be able to continue to protect your son, regardless of his age. Your son is separated from you and is very vulnerable.*
30. *You might wonder how someone manages to find you, get your number etc. Remember! This is someone who can manipulate and charm. He will do anything to get his own way. He will convince people he has a right to speak to his children, a right to enter his 'own home'. A right to speak to you. Be careful who you trust. Also, if it is your friend who is the victim, don't be offended if she won't give you her new number for a while. It is called "keeping myself safe".*

in work, I asked why he didn't tell me and he said he was scared, he was a child for goodness sack, he should never have been scared of a parent. Needless to say, my husband didn't get access.[31]

One of my daughters is still suffering the effects of the abuse, she suffers from trust issues, stress and anxiety. She seen a domestic abuse counsellor in secondary school. She had a breakdown on her 21st birthday, which led to counselling in university because the waiting list for the NHS is far too long. Otherwise they've all grown into the most amazing young adults, my son is the most amazing dad, because he was shown how not to do it, and my daughter is the most amazing mum. Thankfully, they are well grounded adults and I couldn't be prouder of them; they've all done so well for themselves.[32]

And me, well I'm a survivor,[33] it is been 17 years, and in those 17 years, I've brought my children up the best way I could, went to university and got myself a degree. My ex-husband, well he's dead, karma is a bitch. He died three years ago, and then I felt completely free.

---

31. *Child access. A perp will 'fight for his rights'. This is not always about having the children. It is more about making sure you don't have them. It is also a way to further abuse you and try to make sure he still has a reason to have contact with you.*
32. *Disclosure. It is well documented that victims will keep things inside for years before they talk about it. This story is extremely sinister. It is a clear message to the child that the parent will hurt him. It is a control and fear strategy. It is also horrific.*
33. *Ongoing effects. Emotional abuse, any abuse, has long term effects.*

Affirmation

I am enough.
I do not have to change myself to be enough.

Affirmation

Mistakes help me Learn. Failure is a bruise, not a tattoo.

Story Four: Believe in Yourself

The author: The head of a support service for Muslim women experiencing or having experienced domestic violence

I run an online support platform to support Muslim women experiencing domestic violence and healing from violence.

I chose to take the path of healing when I freed myself from a very abusive marriage. During my own healing I have reflected on my story and the reasons I was trapped in domestic violence for over two decades.

I was born into a cycle of intergenerational abuse[1], my parents were so damaged that they believed that our childhood was normal. It was very far from normal, we were on at risk registers not that it made any difference. They saw the social workers as interfering busybodies and put on their best behaviour for visits, those days we were at least fed.

We ended up in the care system[2] due to parental neglect

---

1. All we know when we are little is what is "normal" in our own family. Sometimes we don't realise things that happen are not the same as experiences that other people have.
Violence doesn't breed violence. If you come from a family where violence is regularly a theme, it does not mean that you will continue like that when you are older, unless you want to.
Violence is a choice.
If violence were inherited, then the cycle would mean that women would be violent.
Girls don't generally grow up to be violent.

2. The involvement of social services with a family is stressful. A mother can find her parenting to be "under a microscope". It is not an easy position to be in. Difficult enough to be a victim of abuse without having social workers question you and your responsibility for the safety of the children, and often, not challenge the abusive parent.

and domestic violence, my mother managed to get up back when my father agreed to leave. So my childhood was far from a loving one.

At the age of eighteen I married the first person to ask me,[3] I naively thought he was genuine when he proclaimed his love for me. He was different from anyone I knew, he wanted to marry and was patient to wait for me. I didn't get close to anyone else as they seemed to only want one thing from me and I wasn't going to allow that.

We married, he was gentle, kind, and loving.[4] I was happy, I saw him praying for the first time and became curious as to what could motivate you to pray as certain times. This was far from my life experience, it made me think and want to know more. I asked his friends as he seemed to not be interested in me learning about Islam. He would tell me he loved me as I was and didn't want a Muslim wife. I just wanted to understand what he believed and what made him get up really early and pray. This was spiritual abuse as it interfered with my spirituality or religious practise.

The more I saw him pray, the more I felt a need to know more, then Ramadan came, it was when I saw who he really was. He fasted all day, yet he slept all day and didn't work. Islam was actually rituals and routine something he did but had little connection with.

---

3. *"Only want one thing"....that means sex.*
This lady had been through so much, she only wanted to be loved. She was vulnerable.
Humans need affection to help their emotional growth and mental wellbeing. Without this we suffer.
In abusive situations, a person will crave love, even from someone who is horrible to them.
4. *Intimate relationships are about sharing parts of each other's lives and being open and honest.*
Being denied a part of someone without explanation is not healthy. Denying her access to religious expression is an example of his controlling behaviour.

There was emotional abuse,[5] belittling me through jokes but I just thought he didn't understand it was hurtful.

He controlled my finances and who I saw.[6]

What I wore and the food I ate.[7]

He took me to a sexual health clinic as unknown to me he had infected me with something.[8] I still didn't join the dots.

I just saw it as him loving me so much.[9] He controlled my money and gave me an allowance to spend from my own wages. I saw that as him being better with money than me and helping me.

---

5. Belittling someone and claiming it is "a joke" is abusive. Making a joke of you, if you're not laughing too, is an intention to undermine your confidence and make you feel bad about yourself. An abuser will often make a joke and then, when you react, he will accuse you of being too sensitive, or having no sense of humour.
This isn't true. The truth is, he's deliberately trying to hurt your feelings and doesn't like being called out for doing it, so will blame you.
6. Controlling finances means that you have no choice of lifestyle. If you have no spending power, you have no way to control your standard of living.
Controlling what you wear removes your opportunity to be an individual. Clothing is a very personal choice. You do not owe it to anyone to dress for them. You dress for you.
The situation with clothing is always a lose/lose in an abusive relationship:
Don't show too much skin Cover up; Don't be slutty; Why don't you wear something feminine? Why are you so frumpy?; Show a bit of skin
Dress for yourself. It is your body.
7. Controlling what you eat can be disguised as caring. Maybe they say it is for your better health. It is to control another aspect of your life that should be yours to control. Food is a very emotive issue. It is a basic need. See Maslow's Hierarchy of Needs on *page 102*
8. Sexual health.
One impact of partner infidelity is they can infect you with a Sexually Transmitted Disease.
If your partner doesn't want to use a condom, but is also having sexual intimacy with other people, you are at risk. A huge risk is HIV. Use a condom. If he refuses to use one, that's abusive. Don't let him persuade you that he cannot feel anything when he's wearing one. Over half a billion condoms are purchased globally every year from the worlds No1 condom brand. So don't let him tell you they aren't for him! You need to put your safety first.
9. In a healthy relationship, responsibilities are shared. In a balanced relationship nobody has power over the other person. We can be persuaded what another does for us is "for our own good" because they are better at something than we believe ourselves to be, like managing our money and savings. It may be your partner is better with money, and is fine, as long as you know where your money is going, and you are not being controlled and deprived.
The safest way to prevent financial abuse is to learn about money yourself.

His mother came to live with us in our tiny flat and our marriage died at that point.[10] I was surprised that she also didn't want me to be Muslim. He had a friend called Yousef who supported my desire to be Muslim and gave me books.

I read them and decided I wanted to be a Muslim, I embraced Islam. That's when our issues really began, he was awful until I took my scarf off. I would wear it and remove it this continued for over three years.

Then my mother had a really bad mental breakdown and I had to look after my siblings. I was only 21 and now had five children in my one bedroom flat with my mother in law who hated me.[11]

It was a lot of pressure. He wanted me to put them into care that was not happening.[12]

We were given a social worker and she helped me get a three bedroom flat, he was refusing to move wanting me to choose him and his mother and abandon my siblings. We moved with supermarket trolleys as the new property was not even five minutes' walk. He was so angry.[13]

---

10. When we enter a partnership we become part of another family. This may cause tension. This will be challenging. When others collude with abuse, it can be difficult.
Get to know the family if you can, before you commit.
11. The lady in the story has chosen to convert to Islam and to cover her head. This has no effect on her abuser, but he chooses to punish her because she has done something he disagrees with.
This is really an excuse to be horrible. It could have been anything she did.
12. A cascade of events that resulted in a young woman caring for her five siblings is brutal. Not supporting her in this, knowing what she and they had been through, is spiteful.
Healthy relationships are about supporting each other in difficult times. This case is extreme and taking on the care of five children is a huge responsibility.
More appropriate would be to talk it through, not just have a yes/no scenario.
13. Making you choose:
We are often faced with difficult choices, but forcing people to choose between one person and another is a deliberate strategy what causes this lady to Lose, regardless. It is a Lose/ Lose situation.
It is a similar situation when an abuser wants you to choose between him, or friends. It is a test to see where your loyalty lies.

His mother had her own flat which she was renting and I asked him to take her and himself and leave us if he didn't want to help me raise my siblings.

That marriage ended, as I was a Muslim who wouldn't abandon her family. My mother never recovered and I continued to care for her and my siblings. Two of them reverted to Islam. One year later I remarried.[14]

The second marriage was arranged so I didn't know him, he prayed and wanted a Muslim wife. Upon reflection I was again just seeing the basics rather than who he was as a person. Once again my standards were far too low.[15]

I told everyone proudly I was so happy to marry. What was the chance of someone trying to use me for a passport again? I thought as my ex revealed that's all he wanted me for and time.[16]

I married him and became pregnant very quickly, I thought I couldn't have children as I had none in my first marriage. The red flags were waving, he was not the sweet person I thought he was.[17]

---

14. Remarrying.
Rebound relationships happen when one relationship ends and we quickly get involved with someone else, although we are not emotionally over the first relationship.
15. When we enter a relationship it is always better to know what we want from it. Many people spend more time booking their annual holiday and planning what they are going to do in a fortnight, than they spend time planning a life together.
You need to know what each of you want and your expectations. Marriage is like a contract between two people. If there are things you don't agree with, or things you want that your partner does not want, there will be problems down the line.
16. Both men in this story were foreign nationals and looking for a way to stay in the UK.
So, at the heart of this, they were never looking for a real marriage. They were looking for a Visa.
If you find yourself in a situation where you are being made to marry someone to get them access to your country, please speak to a trusted teacher or contact one of the organizations listed in this book.
17. We all make mistakes. Admitting to them can be embarrassing. Safer to be embarrassed for a little while, than to stay in a bad situation.
**HIGH RISK It is dangerous to leave an abusive relationship. Get support where you can.*

I felt embarrassed that I had chosen so badly and this one was so much worse than the first. He attacked me the day he found out he was to be a father. I removed him from my home but wanted a father for my child therefore believed his constant cry's that he had changed. This continued with him never actually fully living with me as his behaviour was so extreme.[18]

He again used spiritual abuse but in a different way, he wanted me to follow his oppressive version of Islam. He blamed his behaviour on me not being a good Muslim wife.[19]

He constantly misused hadith or the Qur'an to try to manipulate me for his personal gain yet did not meet any of his obligations towards me.[20] When reminded about his responsibilities he would become enraged and tell me he didn't care. For example, he would scream he was the head of the household so I had to obey him in order to be a good Muslim woman who is pleasing Allah.

He swear and curse me by Allah I was going to burn in Hell to get what he wanted.[21] I thought I could avoid rubbing him up the wrong way, blaming his behaviour on my reaction to the abuse. I was broken very quickly and felt trapped, unable

---

18. When he says he'll change...
He won't unless something happens, and he must face consequences. We are what we do, not what we say we'll do.
A person can change but it is not an overnight process.
19. Narcissists never admit responsibility for their abusive behaviours. They will blame you or blame something or someone else. Taking responsibility is not what they do. You cannot fix this. Don't try.
20. Setting standards and religious practices.
Can you dictate to someone if you're not living by that standard yourself? Religion being used to abuse is not religion, it is a smoke screen.
21. Death threats are HIGH RISK behaviour. When someone threatens you like that, take it seriously. This is a way to keep you under control. If you have been threatened, seek help.

to leave. His violence was extreme with constant death threats which were very believable.

One day he broke down in tears because his favourite aunty was murdered by his maternal uncle,[22] his uncle was apparently a good man who lost his temper. He normalised her murder as family problems. I was very afraid he would kill me, I thought he would just flip and I would be gone.

He would isolate me, attack me, slap, swear, insult, scream, break property, hit, push, shove, kick, threaten to kill me with knives, threaten to deface me, burn our home, attack my family.[23]

I reached out for help from his family and the mosque, I was not supported or directed to a domestic violence agency.

They did not have the training to help me.[24] I was alone with a very violent man and I went into survival mode. He always knew I didn't love him or want to be with him and that our intimacy was through coercion. He would be violent or threaten to kill me or those I loved.

I started to study to give me something to focus on, I had left school with no qualifications and worked hard every day despite his constant abuse. I gained a first class honours degree and master's in education, however I also developed fibromyalgia and ended up surviving on medication to numb my feelings and the pain.

---

22. *Women are murdered. This has been the subject of many books. If the murder of females is normalised in your culture, please be careful and seek help. There are organisations that can help you. In some countries, the Honour of the Family puts women at risk.*
23. *All this abusive behaviour is intended to terrify and control.*
24. *There is a list of support agencies at the back of this book. If you find the community you are part of is not supportive, get help from outside. Be aware that seeking help will increase the risk to you from your abuser. Anything that challenges their power and control is dangerous.*

I hated his sexual demands on me the most as my skin crawled when he came near me.[25] I felt like I was breaking apart and wouldn't survive much more.

The day my hell finally ended was just like any other day, he went to the kitchen and inspected it, and he found some grease under the bowl in the sink. He pushed me from one side of the kitchen to the other, he was coming back at me, our son who was nearly 18 was eating his breakfast, and he stood up and shielded me. He told him never to do that again it was just family problems, he shouldn't interfere between man and wife.[26]

Our son walked away quietly, the perpetrator went out and we made a plan to escape him forever. The following week, I made the call that changed everything and reported the abuse. Twenty two years of domestic violence ended. This was the end of my intergenerational abuse, I finally broke my silence, the silence I learned to survive with as a child.

I was terrified to come out of survival mode.[27] In survival mode I was just functioning and became so ill. It was the only way I knew. I then began my healing journey and accepted that I am not what happened to me. I am an individual. I can regain myself outside of my trauma and I am not defined by

---

25. *Unwanted sexual attention is abuse. Nobody is allowed to force you to have sex when you don't want to, even if they say they are because they are your husband. They are not allowed. It is rape.*
26. *When the victim sees the abuses are affecting the children, this may be a pivotal moment in the relationship. When kids step in, it's a huge risk.*
27. *Women report living in "survival mode" for years. If you look at Maslow's Hierarchy of Needs, in the back of the book, you'll see the basic conditions that are necessary for us all. In an abusive relationship even the basic physiological needs are sometimes removed by the perpetrator. Controlling food, clothing, depriving sleep, warmth and safety.*
All the things we need to live at a very basic level.

it. I have acknowledged the abuse I suffered. I spread the word and help people to make the healing journey.

I was still undergoing therapy for my abuse and felt ready to move forward.

My situation at home was still very challenging with my ex-husband stalking me,[28] my children playing up and my fibromyalgia was very bad. Therefore I was looking to escape if I am honest with myself.

I moved forward three years later to marry again.[29] I intended it to be forever, he had love bombed me and mirrored my dreams. I thought I finally found my soulmate, the one written for me. He had a traumatic childhood like me and I thought we were made for each other. He offered me a dream of a life I wanted to live, he was kind thoughtful, complimentary and supportive, or so I thought. It was all a illusion based on lies, a character he created to catch a white revert Muslim wife, someone who he thought he could control. He told me that later, he was yet another perpetrator.

He mainly used emotional and spiritual abuse to try to control me and told me we would be fine so long as I was willing to learn.[30] He wanted me to eat food which wasn't

---

28. Stalking. See definition
Just because a relationship ends, doesn't mean it is over.
There are many instances of ex partners stalking. This is a HIGH RISK behaviour.
Some abusers stalk their victims when they are still in the relationship. Secretly following them to see where they go.

29. A third abusive relationship for this lady. This raises a question:
Do some women attract abusive men? Were you thinking that could be the case?
The answer to this is, abusive men target vulnerable women. We all have periods of vulnerability. A narcissist will actively look for someone he can control.

30. Threats: "We would be fine as long as I was willing to learn"
This is a threat. What would happen if she weren't willing to learn? Going against someone's religious beliefs for absolutely no benefit is very strange behaviour. It is all about control.

halal, relax how I wore my hijab and other things related to the religion. He wanted me to follow his interpretation of Islam, which I clearly would not do.

Everything he told me about himself was a lie,[31] absolutely everything. We married very quickly before I knew who he relay was, he appeared to be a very kind vulnerable person who himself was healing from abuse. I was looking for physical safety and sexual safety, my standards were too low.

He would make cruel jokes mocking my teeth,[32] comment on my height and the fact I had been a victim before.[33]

He moved from being so in love to believing love and intimacy was ego and desire and started to withheld love and intimacy over time.[34] He did this because he wanted me to give him money. He made this very clear, I didn't recognise the person I had married, and he was cold and heartless and only wanted intimacy on his terms without love. The marriage ended when I dared to talk about our issues and asked him to be the man I agreed to marry.

He was so angered that I wanted to address the problems told me Allah took the feelings away.[35] That left me no choice but to walk away after a very short marriage. I choose me.

---

31. Marrying quickly indicates this lady's vulnerability.
He presented as an empathetic person who had experienced similar childhood abuses.
In reality he was a manipulator who targeted her because she was so vulnerable.
32. Cruel jokes about appearance are intended to make you feel undermined and to erode confidence. You are not being sensitive. The jokes really are cruel.
33. When a perpetrator points out you have been a victim before, he is attempting to make the situation your "fault". In fact, the situation is happening because of his behaviour, not yours.
34. Withholding love and intimacy is abusive. It is intended to make you feel unlovable, unwanted and unattractive.
35. Challenging the abuse.
In this situation, he is even blaming Allah, rather than accepting and taking responsibility.

Affirmation

I allow my light to shine.

Affirmation

I treat everyone like they are a someone.

Story Five: Be Brave for Yourself, Not for Others

The author: This lady is now disabled and uses a wheelchair

When I was 16 I lived in a small village. My parents had adopted me and my brother. Back then, you had to be in your 40s before you could adopt, so my parents were what I'd call "an older mam and dad". I was brought up with good and kind values.

I met my ex when I was just 16. I already had a boyfriend, but, when I met my ex, I just thought that he was the "older man" that I was looking for. Or, at least that's what I told myself. Really, he was only 19 at the time.

I regret doing that. My boyfriend at the time is now a happily married, family man. And there's no saying what would have happened between us, but obviously, I do regret what I did because of what came afterwards.

Me and the new boyfriend were together for three years.[1] In that time, he hit me once. He nutted me because I'd said something he wasn't happy with.

1. *Head butting someone is an extremely violent assault. It is not usual to go from no physical violence to such an extreme assault. This is an indicator of this man's ability to be extreme. It was early in the relationship and basically, the intention was to put her in her place.*

One night when we were out,[2] a couple of lads walking passed us had eyed me up. I'm cheeky, so I said to them, "What's the matter, have I got a cabbage for a head?" Just as a joke. No harm intended. My boyfriend went off it and just absolutely beat them up, in the street. Bashing them off the walls and really hurt them.

I knew then what he was capable of doing and I was terrified of him.[3] I knew that if I ever tried to walk away, he wouldn't let me and he wouldn't let me go. I was terrified of him.

He was always controlling. Lots of times I would arrange to have a night with my girlfriends, but at the last minute he would say that he had organised something for him and me and I would have to go along with him.[4]

I would have described him as "not too bad".[5] I was just very aware because I knew what he was capable of. It was

---

2. *Violence towards others.*
In many cases, men who have narcissistic personalities and are violent are only violent to women because they know that the chances of having to answer to any consequences are small. This man is not like that. He is violent to everyone.
3. *Witnessing a person be very violent is a very frightening experience. It is a threat towards you too. You can see what is possible. You know it can happen to you if he feels inclined to do it. It is a removal of your right to feel safe.*
You may remember, when you were little, seeing another child being smacked. How did that feel? Were you afraid too, even though you knew you weren't going to be smacked?
Multiply that by 100 and that's how it feels watching somebody being punched repeatedly.
4. *Isolation is something that happens when someone systematically reduces the amount of contact you have with people.*
He might say things like, "But I want to keep you all to myself",
or, "wouldn't you rather it was just you and me?".
And in this case, there's always the underlying fear of his violence.
Isolation is a HIGH RISK situation.
5. *Let's talk about Minimising.*
Minimising is when we reduce something. When we reduce what someone does it makes it sound less horrible. We are really colluding with the abuser. In this story the lady is kept in fear because she knows what he is capable of. So, as a coping strategy, she is minimising his abusive behaviour.
For example, "he only hit her once". The word ONLY minimises what he did.
Another example, "It was just a slap". The word JUST minimises the violence.

that underlying fear that he would do something horrible if I ever tried to get rid of him.

I didn't realise it at the time, but I was being controlled. I would describe myself as a very strong person, but I didn't see that control at the time.[6]

I knew his dad was abusive to his mam.[7] I knew I didn't want that for me but I was scared.

When I was 19, I got pregnant.

That New Year, me and a friend were at his mam and dads for the party. His dad 'snapped' and he rove his mother all over the house.[8] Her dress was in shreds. I knew I didn't want that for me and my baby. I knew that, as I was having a son, I didn't want my son to be brought up with a dad like that,

---

6. It is a common theme in the stories in this book that the women describe themselves as "strong". And they are! I've spoken to them.
The point is, ANYONE can become a victim of abuse. Whatever your background, you can become that person. Don't blame yourself for that. It is the abuser who abuses.
7. What one person regards as normal, will not be how another person sees it.
The lady in this story knew her abuser's capability for violence and she knew he considered it to be "normal".
8. When we say someone "snapped" we imply they lost control. What is happening is they absolutely are in control.
Why? Because if he had lost control, why didn't he hit someone else at the party? He would have had a few people to choose from.
Why did he choose to hit his wife? To humiliate her. Because he knew she wouldn't hit back. Because he knew there would be no consequences. And, the people who knew him, knew him to be an abuser.
Consider this situation. A man goes to work all day and when he gets home he punches his wife. When asked about it, he says "I just lost control".
A man goes out to work. When he's at work he talks to his colleagues. He calls his wife and she tells him she's at the park with their children and some other parents from the nursery school. He asks "which parents". She replies, "just some of the usual parents at the school. Don't really know them".
He then goes into a meeting and does a presentation in front of his colleagues. It goes well.
On the way home, he stops for an hour at the gym. He speaks to about 10 people when he is there.
He returns home and finds his wife in the kitchen preparing a meal. The children are already in bed.
He asks how it went at the park. She says it was lovely as it was a beautiful, sunny day.
He punches her and tells her not to do that again. Then he tells the police he "Lost Control".
He didn't, did he? He absolutely kept control all the time.

so I decided to end it. I didn't want my son to see me being used as a punch bag.[9]

My dad and his dad were at the house when I told him he had to leave the house we shared. It was then that he ended up in prison for stealing cars. He was always doing that, and he got sent to jail for a few months. That was February or March.[10]

I was a hairdresser. My parents used to look after my son when I was at work. I love hairdressing. I'd wanted to be a hairdresser since I was three or four years old and I absolutely loved it.

I worked weekends and this particular Saturday, in November, I went to work and my mam and dad had the baby.

I wasn't even aware that he'd been let out (of jail).[11] I went home and was in my house. My friend said that my ex had been about and was full of drink.

He came to the house.[12] Everything I know after that comes from medical records, because the next thing I can remember is waking up in hospital.

---

9. This lady was a teenager when she decided to end the relationship. To save her son from seeing what she knew would happen to her, she was extremely brave.
Leaving a relationship is a very dangerous time for the victim. Women are killed AFTER they have left their abuser.
Separation and Pregnancy are both VERY HIGH RISK times.
10. Abusers may be involved in criminal behaviour and known to the police.
11. There seems to be no reliable process of informing people when someone is released from prison. This man was in jail for an offence which wasn't connected to this lady and the violence, even though the lady was at risk from him. There was nothing in place to let her know because the authorities didn't know. Even now, when domestic violence cases go to court, there are occasions when the perpetrator will be released, and the victim doesn't know.
For example, a suspect can apply for Judge in Chambers Bail, and be released and the police don't get the information from the court until the next day.
12. He came to the house.
In that moment he violently assaulted her. He knew she would be there. He knew what he was going to do. It was premeditated.

He violently assaulted me. When my best friend from us being tiny came to see me, she didn't recognise me. My head was so swollen it was as wide as my shoulders.

I've been told that he stood on my neck for so long that I had a stroke. I was 20 years old.

I've been disabled ever since. I'm now in a wheelchair.

He was sent to jail for five years and he was out in two and a half.[13]

I've seen the court papers and statements from the case.[14] In their statements, both him and his mam said that my baby wasn't his.[15]

Of course, there are things that came out of this that I wish hadn't. I've lost the use of one arm, which means that I could not follow my dream of being a hairdresser because I just cannot do it.[16]

There are also good things that have come out of that relationship. I have my son. We adore each other. I am glad that I have him. I have brought him up to have the same values that my parents instilled in me.

I'm a naturally positive person. Always smiling. Goodness knows I need to be!

---

13. There are guidelines that courts follow when sentencing an offender.
This lady is disabled because of the assault. A life sentence for her and her family.
14. Further abuse. It was once considered shameful for a woman to get pregnant before she was married, and in some cultures and religions it is very frowned upon.
By saying the baby isn't his, he is implying the victim was having sex with someone else. Basically, it is Slut Shaming her.
15. His mother is colluding with him, even though she is a victim herself. It may be she was also afraid of him.
16. As a result of this violent assault, she was more than made disabled. He also stole her dream of being a hairdresser.

Authors note about this story

The lady who tells this story is disabled. She dictated it to me because she is not able to write for herself.

I've also spoken to this lady's mum who is now in her 80s. This is what she told me.

"She was a lovely child, but you know, when they get to be teenagers! He was handsome to look at and you would never believe the violence he was capable of. She used to stand up to him. That was the problem. He didn't like it.

I knew he'd hit her once and I'd collared him and said if he did it again it would be me in jail.

We were just astounded. We didn't have this kind of thing in our family. X told me his mam was a victim. His mum was a tiny little thing. You wouldn't believe a big man like his dad would even think to hit her. My husband wouldn't hit a woman. He wouldn't hit a man!

The assault happened on a Friday night. We were looking after the baby, who was nine months old, as X worked weekends as a hairdresser and we had him Friday and Saturday.

The police came at 10pm to say she was in hospital. I went and my husband stayed with the baby.

I've never seen such an horrific sight in all my life.

X was on life support for two weeks and then in intensive care for eight weeks. She couldn't remember anything. She thought the baby was a girl. We used to take him to the hospital and hold him up so she could see him. When she was a bit better, she would come home in her wheelchair at weekends. The physiotherapists were marvellous. It took six years to get her back on her feet.

This affected the whole family. It was like dropping a pebble in a pond. The ripples went on and affected everything.

Our son left home because he couldn't cope with seeing her.

X's care was 24/7. So we had her, and a baby to look after. He was really like our son.

I'm 86 now and I still have to go over to the house and help her.

My husband and I had plans for our retirement that never happened. He was a butcher and planned to sell the business two years later and we were going to get a property in Malta and spend part of our time there because he'd served there and loved it.

That didn't happen. He sold up at the Christmas. People kept coming in and offering to 'take him out', meaning the ex- boyfriend. It really upset my husband. So he sold up. Right at the busiest time of the year.

My husband couldn't go to the court hearing to see what was happening. It affected him a lot.

The ex-boyfriend was charged with attempted murder, but it was reduced to Grievous Bodily Harm with Intent. We were told he could still get a Life sentence for that. He got five years and was out after one year and seven months, because he'd served some of the sentence on remand.

X was a beautiful girl. She was slim with dark hair. Such a lovely personality. Still has a lovely personality. She was very outgoing and full of chatter. Nineteen years old and her life was over."

Affirmation

Good things come to those who work for it.

Additional Resources

Roses are red,
Violets are blue
Don't get with a bloke,
Instead focus on you.

Self Esteem

How we should honour ourselves

One of the things that constantly comes to the surface when talking to people who have been involved with an abuser is their lack of self esteem.

Even the most confident, successful and outgoing women can have their lives eroded to the point where they don't feel like a whole person anymore. Like they are a shadow of their former self.

To make sure this doesn't happen we need to believe in ourselves. We need to feel confident enough to challenge any negative person that steps into our circle.

One way to make sure we are protected is to make a decision about ourselves. And that decision is based on this question:

How am I going to allow someone else to treat me?

Based on your answer, you will know what you are prepared to tolerate from another person.

People will treat you as you allow yourself to be treated.

Sometimes it is difficult to feel good about ourselves. It is certainly not possible to feel 100% good, 100% of the time. Everyone has their off days.

This chapter covers ideas about how to make sure that you grow and develop into the best, confident and self-loving person that you can be.

Self care is not selfish, it is essential. If anyone tells you otherwise, then perhaps that person should not be in your closest circle.

Have a think about how you talk to yourself. Are the things in your head complimentary? Are the things you say out loud caring?

Don't be a victim of negative self talk. Remember who is listening! You!

The list below is some examples of how you can turn some negative self talk into positive self talk:

Do you say this?	Instead, **say this**
I cannot do this	I'm going to give it a try
I'm such a failure than never	I'd rather try and fail try at all
I'm not pretty	I have some really great features
This is too hard	I need to put in a bit more effort
I'm in a bad mood	Today, I'm choosing to be happy
Nothing goes right for me	Dreams can come true
I'm stupid	Most people take a little time to learn stuff
I'm lazy	I feel motivated to act
I'm always getting things wrong	My mistakes help me to learn

Oh, I wish I had better hair/eyes/skin/whatever	I'm perfect just the way I am
I'm useless	I will learn what I can
I'm scared of everything	I will learn to trust myself

Personal Affirmations

Another really good way to put yourself in a positive mindset is to look in the mirror and tell yourself good things out loud. This may feel a little bit strange at first, but once you make it into a daily habit, like brushing your teeth, it will soon become part of your routine.

Try these affirmations and see how you get on...

* *I matter*
* *I choose to be positive What I am doing is enough*
* *I am worthy of my dreams and goals*
* *Today is a good day*
* *I am intelligent*
* *I am a strong and brave person I am good enough*
* *I honour myself*
* *My happiness is mine to own I accept myself for who I am*
* *I am worthy of love and affection Nothing can stop me*
* *Today is going to be fantastic*
* *I can say "No" to others*
* *I can weather this storm I am brave*
* *I am confident*

- *I am getting better every day*
- *Feelings are just visitors I rock, I rock, I rock!*
- *I will succeed today*
- *I am capable of amazing things I allow my light to shine*
- *I am caring*
- *I choose to be happy I choose to be me*
- *Get the idea? How about writing some down for yourself and keeping them somewhere so you can read them every day?*

Gratitude is an Attitude

Starting the day with thoughts of what you are grateful for will give you a positive mindset.

We can all wake up grumpy sometimes, but having grateful thoughts (even in dark times in our life) can give us a glimmer of sunshine, whatever else is going on.

Perhaps a Gratitude Journal would help? Or, even just in your head if you don't want to write it down.

It doesn't have to be a fancy book, a £1 note pad is enough. You can always draw your own doodles and art on it anyway! That would make it even more yours.

Every morning, as you wake, think of five things you are grateful for. It can be absolutely anything, and sometimes, it can be the same thing each day, if that is what helps put you in a better mood.

There are millions of things in the Universe to be grateful for, so I'll only list a few to give you an idea:

Fluffy socks
Sunny days
The seaside
Snow
Lemon ice lollies
Bees
Hair conditioner
The seat in the park
A comfy bed
A hot shower
Birds tweeting
Toothpaste
Beans on toast
Your best friend
Netflix on a Saturday night
Loo roll

The list is literally, endless. You can be grateful for anything.

Think of five things. Smile as you think of them. Feel any better?

Staying Safe

This book is intended to help you recognize if someone is being disrespectful.

Many women go into relationships and don't even realise what is happening to them is abusive. When they do realise, they often feel trapped by their circumstances, or they have no network of people who will support them.

I hope you can use this book and learn what is and is not acceptable.

It is not your job to satisfy him sexually. You are not here to entertain him with photos of you naked. You are not here to do anything that makes you feel uncomfortable

A boner is not a medical condition and it is not your job to cure it.

Don't be scared that not doing the things he wants you to do will make you "lose him". If it means doing things you're uncomfortable with or may regret down the line, he's likely not worth "having" anyway.

Shouting: women shout because they aren't being listened to. Men shout because they aren't being obeyed.

Male privilege isn't about perks and benefits, it is the absence of obstacles.

Talking about abusive relationships is a start to getting things out in the open. It is time to stop the secret nature of domestic abuse and call out those people who commit it.

Don't be a statistic. Know your worth.

Things that we know are very dangerous when someone is in an abusive relationship

Please speak to someone you trust if these things are present in your relationship and you feel concerned.

* *Separation*
* *Pregnancy/new birth*
* *Isolation*
* *Escalation*
* *Stalking*
* *Cultural Issues*
* *Child access disputes*
* *Sexual assault*
* *Suicide threats*
* *Substance use*
* *Child abuse*
* *Controlling behaviour*
* *Animal abuse*
* *Use of weapons*
* *Breaking court orders*
* *Threats to harm*

Maslow's Hierarchy of Needs

Maslow's hierarchy of needs is an idea in psychology proposed by Abraham Maslow in his 1943 paper. "*A Theory of Human Motivation*"

Definitions

Bully: seek to harm, intimidate, or coerce (someone perceived as vulnerable).

Oxford Dictionary

Collude: cooperate in a secret or unlawful way in order to deceive or gain an advantage over others.

Cambridge English Dictionary

Domestic Violence (DV)

Domestic abuse, or domestic violence, is defined across Government as any incident of controlling, coercive or threatening behaviour, violence or abuse between those aged 16 or over who are or have been intimate partners or family members, regardless of their gender or sexuality.

CPS definition

The term 'domestic violence' is capable of bearing several meanings and applying to different types of behaviour which can change and develop over time.

Domestic violence can take many forms: physical injuries caused by punches or beatings, sexual abuse and rape, mental cruelty in the form of humiliation, degradation, bullying, insults or harassment. Frequently, domestic violence is a combination of physical, sexual, psychological and/or emotional abuse. Domestic violence can occur between partners in a relationship, between people living in the same household, between adults and children, or between people who were in a relationship or used to live in the same household.

Shelter definition

At the time of writing, in the UK, the government's Violence Against women and Girls Strategy is being discussed in Parliament.

Gaslighting: Gaslight as expression The psychological term gaslighting, which describes the form of psychological abuse in which the victim is gradually manipulated into doubting their own sanity, originated from the play and its two film adaptations.

Gut feeling or gut instinct: an instinctive feeling, as opposed to an opinion based on facts

Collins Dictionary

Harassment: Harassment is unwanted behaviour which you find offensive or which makes you feel intimidated or humiliated. It can happen on its own or alongside other forms of discrimination. Unwanted behaviour could be spoken or written words or abuse.

Citizensadvice.org.uk

Love: An intense feeling of romantic attachment based on an attraction felt by one person for another; intense liking and concern for another person, typically combined with sexual passion.

Oxford Dictionary

Male privilege: male privilege is the system of advantages or rights that are available to men solely on the basis of their sex. A man's access to these benefits may vary depending on how closely they match their society's ideal masculine norm.

Wikipedia

Mansplaining: the explanation of something by a man, typically to a woman, in a manner regarded as condescending or patronizing.

Oxford Dictionary

Minimise: reduce (something, especially something undesirable) to the smallest possible amount or degree.

Oxford Dictionary

Misogyny: hatred, dislike, or mistrust of women, manifested in various forms such as physical intimidation and abuse, sexual harassment and rape, social shunning and ostracism, etc.

Ingrained and institutionalized prejudice against women; sexism.

Dictionary.com

Narcissist: a person who has an excessive interest in or admiration of themselves.

"narcissists who think the world revolves around them"

Oxford Dictionary

Patriarchy: a system of society or government in which the father or eldest male is head of the family and descent is reckoned through the male line.

- a system of society or government in which men hold the power and women are largely excluded from it.
- a society or community organized on patriarchal lines.

Oxford Dictionary

Slut shaming: slut-shaming is the practice of criticizing people, especially women and girls, who are perceived to violate expectations of behaviour and appearance regarding issues related to sexuality.

Wikipedia

Stalking: stalking is a pattern of repeated behaviour that includes unwanted attention, contact, harassment, or other conduct towards a specific person. Stalking behaviours may be committed in person, by following the victim, or by monitoring and harassing the victim electronically. Both men and women are victims of stalking all over the world. To explore this concept, consider the following stalking definition.

Legaldictionary.net

Torture: the action or practice of inflicting severe pain or suffering on someone as a punishment or in order to force them to do or say something.

Oxford Dictionary

Additional Support

* *In an emergency call 999 for the police*
* *Womensaid.org.uk*
* *Refuge.org.uk*
* *Citizensadvice.org.uk*
* *Victimsupport.org.uk*
* *Childline.org.uk*
* *Shelter.org.uk*
* *karmanirvana.org.uk*

About the Author

Rie Pearson was a police officer for 27 years. During that time, she was told to do the job of being the Domestic Violence Officer.

Back in the 1990, the DV Officer was normally the pregnant police woman at that station. This was when female police officers were still quite rare in the UK.

PC Pearson did not want the job. At the time, she was still enthusiastic about kicking doors in and the excitement of working on the front line. The DV role (in the 1990s) was very different to what it is now.

At that time, after a DV incident, the DV officer would re-contact the victim and talk her through her options. It was not very focused on bringing the offender to justice, because back then, these type of incidents were not really regarded as crime unless there was an assault. PC Pearson thought it was both patronizing (it was) and didn't result in many successful convictions (it didn't, but that's another tale).

However, as in any hierarchy, a police constable has to follow instructions and the officer found herself looking at the statistics.

And so began her journey of learning and working with both victims and offenders.

She began by looking at other offending behaviours and found that about 70% of the abusers were already involved in other crime.

The Safer Families Project was the first holistic service to work with offenders, their victims and children in the UK. After securing a role on the Project (basically begged her boss to let her get involved) she worked with offenders to address their abusing. The participants did not know she was a police officer.

This was then followed by a job at Police Headquarters where she worked in the Community Engagement Department. This involved working on a multi force project to assess the information from previous domestic murders and develop a Risk Assessment Tool to be rolled out across all forces in the UK for use at all DV incidents.

Then came three years in the Crime Department Public Protection Unit, to work strategically on policy, procedure and guidance for the force.

Rie Pearson is married with three children and she lives in north east England.

How to connect with Rie:

www.riepearson.com
Instagram: @bekindnoexcuses